The Sporting Life
Guide to Owning a Racehorse

In this book, George Rae addresses the complexities of the arcane and idiosyncratic world of the Turf on behalf of the present or would-be racehorse owner. Buying a horse, appointing the trainer, documentation, fees and expenses, prize money, the organisation and structure of racing, its labyrinthine rule book, veterinary matters, insurance, breeding, selling and a host of other topics relevant to the experience of ownership are lucidly and candidly explained in practical detail.

The author is a racing correspondent of *The Times* and contributor on racehorse matters to the specialist sporting press.

The Sporting Life

Guide to

Owning a Racehorse

By George Rae

©1990 George Rae

First published 1990 by The Sporting Life
Orbit House, 1 New Fetter Lane, London EC4A 1AR

ISBN 0 901091 25 1

Cover origination by Reprosharp Ltd, London EC1
Text typeset by Cotswold Typesetting Ltd, Cheltenham
Cover printed by Stones the Printers, Banbury, Oxon
Text printed by The Eastern Press Ltd, Reading, Berks

Cover photograph
Jubilant owner Sirrell Griffiths and 100/1 winner
Norton's Coin in the media spotlight after the 1990
Cheltenham Gold Cup (photo: The Sporting Life)

Acknowledgement
The author expresses thanks to the many who
generously gave their time and expertise to help in the
preparation of this book

For my parents

CONTENTS

Contents

1: First principles

To own a racehorse is to buy shares in the optimism business. As John Biggs, Director-General of the Racehorse Owners' Association (ROA), succinctly puts it: 'An owner may have as much hope as he likes, but no expectation.'

It is worth remembering. Embarking upon racehorse ownership on the assumption of it being financially profitable is to court almost certain disappointment, if not disaster. The equation of ownership in Britain does not balance, nor will it for the foreseeable future.

What you choose to lay out for your horse is, of course, your own business. Once you have become an owner in circumstances other than joining a racing club, you should be thinking in terms of a total annual outlay in the region of £12,000 for that mythical 'average horse', although there will be variations depending on which trainer you choose.

There are also enormous regional differences. The major southern centres of Newmarket, Lambourn and Epsom are likely to be more expensive than less fashionable areas. The argument of getting what you pay for cannot be totally ignored but there is still room for manoeuvre.

To place a horse with a leading Newmarket trainer will leave little change out of £20,000. That, however, is the equivalent of

1

Harrods. Fine, if you can afford it, but no cause for despair if not. Take the opportunity to shop around. There are plenty of capable trainers in what may patronisingly be called the provinces.

The end of 1989 and the beginning of 1990 produced two decisions, the impact of which on training fees, and therefore ownership costs, will take time to assess thoroughly. The first, an up to 25 per cent increase in stable lads' wages, was swiftly followed by a new business rating system which is also likely to increase charges. Racing must also digest the effects of the poll tax on an often migratory workforce. Trainers will pass on at least some of the rises, but more than ever the onus is on the owner to be sure of his likely outlay.

Be aware, too, of the unexpected: perhaps more entries than were originally envisaged, the abortive journeys to abandoned meetings, veterinary bills and so on. There is also the spectre of the write-off. One owner paid 15,000 guineas for a yearling and invested a further £10,000 in its upkeep before, a year later and without it ever having seen a racecourse, it was re-offered at public auction and fetched just 1,500 guineas. Accidents do not always happen to someone else.

On the other side of the equation, do not expect miracles of prize-money levels. The ROA quotes odds of 20/1 against an owner making his racing pay. Some 50 per cent of owners do not win a single penny.

Even the big battalions of the Maktoum brothers from Dubai, Robert Sangster, the Aga Khan and Prince Khalid Abdullah cannot hope to make racing pay through prize-money alone. Their respective empires, even founded as they are on the most celebrated bloodlines, include too many moderate horses to soak up the relatively meagre winnings of the successful. At that level, the path away from red ink lies in producing top-class racehorses who retire to stud. It is the stallion careers of the Nashwans and Dancing Braves of this world, and the millions in fees they generate, which keep racing's dreadnoughts afloat.

The only sensible route to involvement is in pursuit of the pleasure, camaraderie and sheer good fun that close contact with racing can bring. Shared enthusiasm cuts through the divisions of society, for a few hours at least. The lord, the stable lad, the millionaire and the tout are drawn together by the addictive fascination with what is to many man's noblest creation: the Thoroughbred.

High or low, no-one is immune from racing's roller-coaster: one minute glorious triumph, the next unmitigated disaster. The dictum 'All men are equal on the Turf, and under it' may not be strictly true, but its sentiment is unmistakable. Despite the financial demands, racehorse ownership has become more accessible in recent years. The growth in partnerships, and more especially the mushrooming racing clubs, have created opportunities on an unprecedented scale. Enthusiasm, rather than enormous wealth, is now the prerequisite of participation on the Turf.

Both in these pages and generally, racing is referred to as a sport, but in reality it is a complex multi-million pound industry employing perhaps a hundred thousand people. There are around 14,000 horses in training in Britain and some 11,000 owners. There has been a slight upward trend in the numbers of owners, about 18 per cent over the past five years, largely accounted for by the fact that partnerships must now be comprised of registered owners, and also a growth in company ownership.

About 30 per cent of owners leave racing annually to be replaced by an almost identical figure. There are any number of reasons for the exodus. Many, probably after suffering a couple of years without success, are driven away by disappointment. Some find the financial burden too great. Others discover that it was not as much fun as they had expected.

There has also been a discernible change among the hard-core ownership. As costs escalate, the sole owner is looking to spread the risks involved and is more likely to take shares in a series of horses rather than commit himself to one individual.

It is simplistic to say that racing is a great leveller. Money talks and, when it does, it speaks volumes. But there is still room for the small owner. Look no further than Sirrell Griffiths, the Welsh dairy farmer who carried off the Cheltenham Gold Cup in 1990 with Norton's Coin.

Griffiths, in his capacity as breeder, owner, trainer and general dogsbody, drove Norton's Coin to the races, saddled him, and then watched as he silenced the packed legions of the Desert Orchid fan club. Dreams do sometimes come true.

But a big-race win is not the only cause for celebration. Top-class horses, after winning great races, are all too often led in by straight-faced men in sombre suits, looking as though they have just been handed a singularly unpleasant chore. Contrast that with the reception afforded a humble selling plater returning to the joyous war whoops of delighted connections.

Not all ownership is motivated by spotless love of the game. Putting one over on the bookmakers is a powerful attraction to all followers of racing. To many owners, the thundering hooves, flashing colours and bobbing jockeys are incidental to the serious business of landing a gamble. How better to do that than from the inside? With the right information, the thinking goes, all those days when the bookmakers had the last laugh can be set to rights.

Ownership is a marvellous conversation piece, although the audience may not always appreciate your fervour. One excited woman owner regaled her hairdresser with the minutiae of a newly-acquired horse, ending the monologue by describing the object of her affections as a bay. 'Oh,' said the hairdresser, under-standing finally dawning, 'you mean it's a brunette.'

Participation is the cornerstone of ownership, so try not to have it blighted by ignorance. Racing still clings lovingly to a certain mystique: the use of obscure terminology, its labyrinthine rule book, the whispered instructions, that sense of it all being rather more complicated than it actually is. Do not be intimi-dated, nor be afraid to ask. What you fear may be interpreted as stupidity is a feeling shared by thousands of others, many experi-enced in racing. So, at whatever stage of ownership you find yourself, make it a rule to ask, ask and ask again.

Different seasons

Racing is divided into Flat and National Hunt, which is in turn sub-divided into hurdling and steeplechasing. Most people have a leaning towards one or the other and will consequently find it more enjoyable to be part of that environment.

First principles

There is an historical rivalry, mostly good-humoured, between the opposing factions of sporting jump fans and money-grubbing supporters of Flat racing. The financial rewards of Flat racing are superior, disproportionately so higher up the scale. In 1989, Nashwan won in excess of £500,000 in just two races, the Derby and the King George VI & Queen Elizabeth Diamond Stakes – a total of little more than five minutes' work. The ever-popular Desert Orchid required more than 60 races even to approach that figure in win and place prize-money!

Aside from prize-money considerations, be clear about your views of going racing. If the thought of a cold, rain-lashed winter's day is hell, National Hunt racing is unlikely to be your cup of tea.

Following the introduction of all-weather racing in the autumn of 1989, the Flat season is officially the calendar year, from January to December. However, the vast majority still consider the Flat to run along its traditional lines, from the Lincoln Handicap meeting at Doncaster in late March until the November Handicap fixture at the same course early in November.

The calendar sometimes dictates that Doncaster does not start the ball rolling, usually when Easter falls early in the year. On those occasions, the season begins at several courses simultaneously.

The National Hunt season is somewhat longer, running from the end of July until early in June the following year. The close season lasts less than two months.

It is relatively simple to find out when meetings are staged. The Jockey Club fixture list is agreed well in advance and is widely incorporated into diaries, wall calendars and the racecourses' own publicity material, as well as being thoroughly publicised in the press.

Flat and National Hunt racing, though related, are fundamentally different and demand contrasting qualities of their respective performers. Flat racing places its greatest emphasis on speed and precocity, while National Hunt racing demands endurance and agility.

Horses can begin racing as two-year-olds – all horses celebrate their birthday on 1 January regardless of their actual date of foaling – first over 5 furlongs and then over gradually longer distances. Two-year-olds, often called juveniles, are not allowed to run more than 5 furlongs before the York May meeting, more than 6 furlongs before Royal Ascot in June, and more than 7 furlongs before the York August meeting. They can then tackle progressively further, until by the end of the season they are allowed to run at up to a mile-and-a-quarter.

At three years old and over, Flat horses race from distances ranging from 5 furlongs to around two-and-threequarter miles. The Classics, the owner's Holy Grail, are run from the straight mile of the 1,000 and 2,000 Guineas to the 1 mile 6 furlongs and 127 yards of the St Leger. The Derby is contested over a mile-and-a-half, and its influence has moulded middle-distance racing, making a mile-and-a-quarter to a mile-and-a-half the glamour sector of Flat racing.

Horses are eligible to run over hurdles from the latter half of their three-year-old career – that is, as soon as the new National Hunt season begins. At this stage they, too, are described as juveniles, it being their first season over jumps. From that starting point they may remain hurdling or be sent over fences. Although a distinction is made between Flat and National Hunt horses, many National Hunt runners will have moved on from the Flat to jumping, or often continue to race under both codes.

The laying out of hurdles and fences is controlled by Jockey Club regulations. For hurdle races, there must be at least 8 hurdles in the first 2 miles, with a flight for each additional quarter of a mile. In a chase, there must be at least 12 fences in the first 2 miles, and at least 6 fences in each succeeding mile. There should be at least one open ditch for each mile, although water jumps are now optional.

2: Types of ownership

What type of owner do you want to be? Perhaps, more pertinently, what type can you *afford* to be? Unless money is no object, the owner must balance economics against the power of his voice.

There are five basic forms of ownership:

sole ownership
partnership
leasing
company ownership
racing clubs

The more people involved, the more the costs will be shared, but the individual's say will be reduced correspondingly. The sole owner has no-one to argue with over the horse's programme, apart, perhaps, from the trainer. Partnerships, however, must be guided by discussion. Members of racing clubs can expect to have almost no voice in where the horses run, no matter how keen an interest they take.

The deciding factor is likely to be money. The sole owner must pick up all the bills as the price of his independence. Partnerships are quite likely to be framed with finances in mind. A bewildering variety of racing clubs offer the opportunity of ownership for a

relatively low outlay, and the club member knows precisely what his outgoings will be.

Sole ownership

This remains the most popular form of ownership despite its attendant financial demands. Although the days when ownership was confined largely to the aristocracy are gone, having a race-horse to yourself remains the province of the wealthy man. Yet even here there is a grading between what may be termed the comfortably well-heeled and the exceedingly rich.

The growth of racing internationally over the last two decades has strengthened the hand of those in the first division, particularly among the super-league owners characterised by the Arabs.

After the balance of power in the breeding industry had shifted from Britain to the United States, it was the mega-wealthy who were able to buy the world's finest bloodstock at the prestigious Keeneland Sales in Kentucky. Much of that bloodstock has returned to Britain to make the standard of racing here the highest in the world. Although such a policy has inevitably produced its share of backfires (mention of the $10.2 million Snaafi Dancer, who never even made it to the racecourse, is guaranteed to raise a snigger), the overall record is an ever-growing list of Classic winners. The seat of turf domination is among the high-rolling sole owners.

Partnership

A partnership can range from 2 to 12 persons. Within that regulation, the composition of the partnership may vary at will. The partners do not have to have equal shares. One partner may, for example, account for 50 per cent, with the remaining 50 per cent being divided in variable amounts between a variable number of people. To take it to its extreme conclusion, one partner may have 89 per cent of the partnership with 11 individuals making up the balance at 1 per cent each. Additionally, a company may be involved in a partnership, nominating an authorised agent to act on its behalf as one of the partners.

The bills are paid in accordance with the size of the share of the partnership, and a partner's say in a horse's career, although

9

more difficult to quantify, is also likely to carry more weight the greater the share. All the partners will, however, have a hand in the making of decisions.

The partners must be 'registered owners', and the other formalities of ownership – registration of colours, of the horse's name, of a training agreement and an authority to act – must be observed. Partnerships must be registered with the Jockey Club before the horse runs, and will be allowed only in horses which have been named. The registration procedures are described in detail in Chapter 5.

One partner must be nominated as the person in whose name the horse will be entered. When it has been entered or has run in that name it must continue in the same name until the end of the calendar year. The horse will also run in the colours of that person, and only he need have his colours registered. However, all the partners, regardless of their share, must sign a training agreement, although only one of the partnership has to sign an authority to act.

Entries will be accepted in the name of any one of the partners once the partnership is registered. The cost of registering a partnership is £16.50 plus VAT*.

Instead of one partner being nominated, the alternative is to register a partnership name under which the activity of the partnership will be conducted. For example, the members of a local football team may prefer to have their horse running under the banner of 'Rovers Racing' rather than in the name and colours of one individual.

To register a partnership name, which costs £55 plus VAT, the names and addresses of the partners, and the partnership name, must be provided.

The partnership, or extended partnership to use its full title, has superseded the syndicate, which was in danger of falling expensively foul of potential problems raised by the Financial Services Act. The main difference is that, in a syndicate, the horse was leased to usually three or four people, and only they had to be registered as owners. The remaining members, at least for the

*Throughout this book, charges quoted are those prevailing at time of writing (July 1990).

purposes of Jockey Club administration, did not exist.

In a partnership, the part-owners are liable for each other. Should one or more fail to pay, the extra burden must then be shared among the other partners. The onus is not on the Jockey Club or Weatherbys to pursue defaulters on your behalf. Should it happen, the terms of the partnership registration, which makes provision for such an unfortunate eventuality, will be politely pointed out to you.

Therein lies the golden rule of partnerships. Only enter into them with people you know and trust. Be aware of the danger of answering advertisements offering shares in horses. The resulting partnerships could easily throw you together with people you do not know and may never meet. You are acting in good faith but the same may not be true of everybody else.

A newcomer interested in a partnership should explore the possibilities of recruiting an existing owner. His experience of getting the most out of ownership will be invaluable and there is the extra incentive of learning from his mistakes.

Where a partnership includes more than four people, all charges and payments will be made through the partner in whose name the horse is entered. It will then be up to the partners to take steps to divide those charges and prize-money among themselves.

While partnerships can help reduce the costs of ownership, they can also be a good way to make former friends. The euphoria of buying and putting a horse in training can quickly give way to powerful stresses and disagreements among the partners. Will it run at Newmarket this week or Haydock next week? Should it run at a different distance? Do we risk it on firm ground? The scope for argument is immense and, by default, most people end up going along with the trainer's wishes. However, what the trainer wants may not coincide with what other people want, so it is worth trying to devise some form of friendly decision-making apparatus among the partners, and with the trainer, in advance. It may not cover all eventualities but it should prevent at least some dissension in the ranks.

While you thrash out your thoughts on consultation, never lose sight of the fact that the horse's best interests should be paramount. The time to run any horse is when it is in peak condition, and that cannot be guaranteed to fit in with all the partners all the time. Be sensible, and flexible, enough to let the horse take the right opportunity when it arises.

The trainer, portrayed here as a third-party, may be directly involved as one of the partners. Prospective owners often glow at the prospect of having the trainer as a partner. He is someone else with whom to share the cost, and naturally he must have faith in the horse if he wants to be a partner. That is not necessarily the case.

Training is not only about winners, it is also a numbers game. The numerical strength of the yard needs to be kept up to make the operation viable. A trainer may, therefore, have shares in a series of horses simply to have them in the yard. It does not automatically follow that he believes every one to be a potential Derby or Cheltenham Gold Cup winner.

However, the real problems arise if disagreements break out among the partners. Serious arguments are damaging in any partnership but the difficulties are magnified when the trainer puts on his owner's hat. If there is dissatisfaction with the way things are going, there is always the option to move the horse to another trainer. But when the trainer is a partner, the last thing he will approve is the horse going elsewhere.

The avenues are to leave the horse where it is and risk festering discontent, or to try to buy the trainer's share. Buying inevitably involves a valuation, and, as human nature unfailingly demonstrates, buyers and sellers rarely share the same thoughts on price. If a compromise can be reached, so much the better. There is, though, the danger that the horse may have to be offered at public auction to resolve the dispute. If you ever attend a bloodstock auction, notice how many lots are offered 'to dissolve a partnership'. Not all splits are acrimonious, and they most certainly do not all involve trainers, but it is a fact of life that people fall out.

The sale produces an unarguable valuation in the selling price, and the money received would then be distributed among the warring factions in proportion to their shares in the horse. Remember, though, that sending the horse to auction puts it in the public domain. If several of the partners wish to buy it back they must face all-comers, including the trainer or any dissatisfied partner keen to retain ownership.

Although trouble is the last thing in people's minds when they form partnerships, a legal agreement between the partners is advisable (solicitors in the racing centres of Newbury and Newmarket are well placed to offer guidance). Not all the questions raised will be of the purely racing variety and some may have far-reaching consequences for the partnership. If a partner wants to pull out, should his share be automatically offered to the remaining members or should the partnership be disbanded and reformed? Who will have the final say when to sell the horse?

The Jockey Club's position is clear. 'In the event of a dispute between partners which they are unable to resolve, legal advice should be taken as the Jockey Club cannot mediate in such matters' says eye-catching bold type on the back of the partnership registration form. The message is obvious: if the partners start fighting, do not expect the Jockey Club to referee.

Under the partnership agreement, a part-owner cannot assign his share without the consent of his partners. Any changes mean that a fresh partnership must then be registered. The Racing Calendar Office at Weatherbys must be notified when a partnership is terminated, even when the horse is sold at public auction. Termination is official only after notice has been received from one of the partners on behalf of the partnership, or from the authorised agents of all the partners. A horse which was the property of a syndicate is ineligible to run until the required notification of termination has been lodged. The details of partnerships and terminations are published in the *Racing Calendar* (the official journal of the Jockey Club) each week.

Leasing

An alternative to buying a horse is leasing. In simple terms, you have the horse for the duration of its racing career or the length of time specified in the lease, and the lessor retains ownership. You have the fun of racing without the capital outlay.

Historically, breeders tended to sell their colts and retain their

fillies for future breeding purposes. Although that trend is changing nowadays with studs moving towards a policy of selling the
greater part of their production regardless of sex, there are still
leasing opportunities to be had to the advantage of both sides.

The lessee does not have to find a lump sum for the horse,
while the lessor can find out at someone else's expense if a filly
he intends to breed from has any ability.

The agreement is not exclusive to fillies. For example, if an
owner has little interest in Flat racing he could lease a colt for its
Flat career and have him back when it is time to race over jumps.
Or if a trainer has a horse running in his own name he may be
prepared to lease it.

Contacting potential lessors is best done through a bloodstock
agent or trainer. Professional help is vital here because if you
have little knowledge of conformation or pedigrees you could be
taken for a ride. A reputable agent should have his finger on the
pulse of movements in the bloodstock market and, by regularly
attending the sales, be aware of avenues worth exploring.
Trainers, too, move in the same circles and should be able to
assist.

If you are keen to investigate the possibilities of leasing on
your own behalf, you could try writing to some of the leading
studs – the *Directory of the Turf* carries a relevant section – for
information about their policy. If they are interested, it is still
worth taking your expert along.

A leasing agreement must be confirmed by a Registration of
Lease lodged with the Jockey Club. It sets out the date from
which the lease becomes effective and either a date on which it
will terminate or the option to terminate. Should the lease be left
open-ended, only the lessee can terminate. This is to protect the
lessee, who, should he be fortunate enough to lease a horse
which becomes top class, may otherwise find the horse being
taken away by the lessor on the eve of a big race.

Under the leasing agreement, the lessee undertakes to 'pay all
entrances, stakes, forfeits and other expenses' and agrees to
return to the lessor a mutually agreed percentage of prize-money
won. The Jockey Club is reluctant to suggest a precise figure,
preferring instead to assess each agreement individually.

However, the Jockey Club likes to see a 'reasonable' percentage retained by the lessee and, if the prize money returned is heavily weighted in favour of the lessor, the Jockey Club may refuse to register the lease.

A lease must also observe the basics of ownership. It cannot be registered for horses whose names are not registered and the lessee or lessees must be registered owners. Should the lessees form a partnership, it must be registered in accordance with the rules relating to them. It costs £16.50 plus VAT to register a lease.

This is written primarily with the potential lessee in mind, but should you be a potential lessor remember that the Jockey Club and Weatherbys are not responsible for the collection of any moneys due. It is up to you to make certain that you receive what is yours. Also, the lessor should be aware that he can withhold permission to run a horse in a selling or claiming race, where it may be bought by an outside party.

At the termination of the lease, the lessee agrees to return the horse 'free of all expense'. Any costs incurred up to that point are the concern of the lessee. Should a horse already be in training, it can be leased with its existing engagements.

Company ownership

Company ownership is best founded on the desire to advertise or promote the company in question. Racecards nowadays are liberally sprinkled with the names of horses reflecting either the company which owns them or the products in which they specialise. The Edinburgh Woollen Mill has, for example, been successfully represented by a series of good-class National Hunt horses bearing the 'Tartan' prefix. Schweppes has also been involved with such as Schweppeshire Lad and Schhh You-Know-Who.

Advertising through racing, runs the argument, gives the company a higher profile. Its name will automatically be seen in the race programmes carried by the national newspapers and seen on television. Customers will therefore tend to follow the horse when it runs.

The ultimate advertising value is, of course, determined by the success of the horse. If it wins consistently, it will keep its owner in the news. If it always figures among the also-rans, it comes to fewer people's attention.

A word of warning here. If the principal reason for embarking on company ownership is the thought of recovering some of the costs of purchase and training through revenue taxation and VAT allowances, be aware of the risks. No-one needs reminding that the Inland Revenue and Customs & Excise are formidable opponents. You may escape for several years, but retribution is probably only delayed.

The best move is to take expert advice. Look first at accountants based around the major training centres. They are more likely to be familiar with the difficulties specific to this field. Another possibility is for the company accountant to discuss the position with the Racehorse Owners' Association, which has considerable first-hand experience in this field. It should be stressed that advice needs to be taken before a horse is purchased if lost causes are to be avoided.

That is not to say, however, that the authorities are bound to throw out every case which comes before them. As a general rule, a company, or an individual for that matter, cannot obtain tax relief for racing expenses. Only when the Inland Revenue and Customs & Excise accept that a horse is kept wholly and exclusively for purposes of business can a company owner claim the costs incurred in keeping the horse.

That is not so much the golden rule as the only rule. If it cannot be shown that the horse is solely an advertising vehicle, the prospects of success are slim. Once ownership looks like being for the benefit of one of the directors, rather than the company as a whole, you will be on a very sticky wicket. Tax inspectors must be satisfied that the expenses are legitimately incurred in the pursuit of business, rather than a director's hobby.

A company's case can, in fact, be made more difficult if a director is an existing racehorse owner. The authorities, having evidence of his enthusiasm, may look less favourably on the company if it suddenly begins to acquire a string of racehorses in its own name. That goes double if a director reduces his personal racing interest concurrently with his company increasing its holding. The inference is obvious and the authorities are unlikely to miss the point.

Ideally, the decision to purchase a horse should be shown in the company's minutes to be that of a group of people, the board of directors perhaps, rather than just one man. The decision should also be seen to be based on recognisable economic principles.

The company may have to demonstrate that costs are in line with the advertising policy. A company with an advertising budget which generally runs to £15,000 will need to put a persuasive case for adding two horses, and perhaps £30,000, to its bill. For that reason, the biggest companies have least problems in obtaining relief. The multinationals have such mammoth advertising budgets that the addition of a couple of horses to promote further a company name is likely to be considered well within the existing framework.

Evidence may also be required that the advertising is likely to generate business. For example, running the horse regularly at televised meetings would enable a company's name to reach a wider audience. Remember that horses' names can be changed only in strictly limited circumstances, so it is important to buy unnamed stock if you want the horse to advertise the company through its name. However, it will not automatically damn the case if a horse fails to carry the company name. Indeed, some companies actively refuse to name a horse after themselves in case it turns out to be useless.

Keep in mind the general principles of bloodstock purchasing, though. It is all very well thinking that the company may be best represented by three-mile chasers running through the winter, but that type of horse hardly ever comes ready-made and will almost certainly already be named. You will need plenty of money and patience while the horse develops, whereas a two-year-old will be unnamed and generally set to race reasonably soon.

Be particularly wary of citing entertaining as a reason for ownership. That never goes down well and could easily sink the case single-handedly.

The old saw about every case being treated on its merits by the relevant authorities is particularly true here. There are no legal

precedents to call upon for guidance, and the Inland Revenue is not in the business of offering opinions on hypothetical cases. There is no point telephoning and offering the 'A friend of mine' gambit. Your case will be judged entirely on the evidence you present when the time comes.

Should a company qualify for tax relief, prize-money and any profit on the sale of the horse will be taxable. If no relief is claimed, prize-money and profits will be tax-free.

If, having mulled over the options, the decision is taken to become a company owner, it is necessary to register with the Jockey Club as a recognised company. The names and addresses of all the directors and the company secretary are required, as are the name and address of the company's bankers. Details of previous ownership experience of either directors or secretary are also requested.

Registration will be denied if any of the directors or the secretary is a disqualified person, and additionally the Jockey Club requires the company's Memorandum and Articles of Association, the Register of Members, the latest annual report, and the latest balance sheet and profit-and-loss account. The registration fee is £275 plus VAT.

The company must also appoint an authorised agent, usually the trainer, to act on its behalf under the Rules of Racing.

Racing clubs

The spread of racing clubs has been the greatest single change in ownership patterns in recent years. Many people who had previously found direct involvement in racing beyond their means are now able to participate through a plethora of clubs.

It is, in fact, inaccurate to call them clubs. They are actually limited companies in which people are invited to buy shares. Those who buy shares are not owners in the strict sense of the word – they do not have to be registered with the Jockey Club – but shareholders in a company which owns and runs horses.

Once the shares have been bought, that is the extent of the outlay. The shareholders' liability is limited and no further call can be enforced. That is a worthwhile safety net, not available with other forms of ownership. Having paid once, there will not be a steady drain on finances if things start to go wrong.

The club is established for a fixed period, usually between one and two years, and, at the end of that time, will be dissolved. The assets of the company, principally winnings and any proceeds from the sale of horses, will be distributed among the shareholders, less any outstanding administrative charges. The club is then likely to be reformed, with the existing shareholders given first choice in the new recruiting drive.

The theory of racing clubs is that, by bringing together large numbers of people – perhaps thousands – and pooling their resources, each can enjoy the thrills of involvement at a limited cost. That, of course, is the positive side. On the other hand, an individual shareholder will have no say in the placing of the company's horses in particular races or at which courses they run.

Just how big a limitation that becomes is largely in the members' own minds. If a member is committed to the club and its horses, he is unlikely to be unduly bothered by the fact that the day-to-day decisions are out of his hands. As far as he is concerned, he is an owner as much as anyone. He will gain great satisfaction from watching the horses run and regaling his friends with stories of his involvement in the Sport of Kings.

There, perhaps, is the key. Attitude is paramount, no less than in any other area of ownership. The more positively you think, the more you will get out of racing. If your sense of ownership is dominated by the belief that you really own three hairs in the horse's tail, then your dream of racehorse ownership is not fulfilled. Think positively. Of course you are an owner: who can say otherwise?

The possible levels of investment range from a couple of hundred pounds at one end to five-figure sums to be a part of a more highly-funded operation. There will be no problems finding subjects for study as the clubs are advertised extensively in newspapers, particularly the sporting press, and on the television information services, usually on the pages dealing with racing.

The best course of action is to write or telephone for as many prospectuses as possible. The prospectus will set out the aims of the company and its costs, how many horses it intends to have and with which trainers. It should also say how many shares are on offer and the share price, so you know how many fellow members you will have, assuming the offer is fully subscribed. It will also remind you that it is a highly speculative investment. The common denominator is the salesman's hyperbole. All clubs will tell you how they use leading trainers and top-flight jockeys, even if closer examination shows they are barely on nodding terms with the winner's enclosure.

It is vital to be selective. Even if the main aim is to have a bit of fun, the enjoyment will be greatly increased by associating with a winning team. Do not be afraid to ask the club how many winners it had in the most recent season, and how its past record shapes up.

Look particularly at the longer established clubs. The fact that a club has been around for several years suggests it has at least some sort of track record. Shareholders will not continue to sign on with a club which has virtually no winners, and for that reason it is not uncommon to see unsuccessful clubs failing to attract sufficient shareholders when they attempt to reform.

Check out trainers' and jockeys' success rates. If you take a close interest in racing you will soon recognise those trainers and jockeys doing better than others. If not, most newspapers regularly carry tables of the leaders either on the Flat or over jumps. Should you wish to dig a little deeper, the weekly Timeform 'black book' (on sale at racecourses and in sporting bookshops) carries a record of how many winners trainers and jockeys have had in previous years.

It is also worth investigating the composition of the club's string. Ideally it should have a mixed squad of Flat and National Hunt horses so that there is plenty of interest throughout the year. Be sure, too, that you know the geographical location of the club's trainers. When stable tours are organised by the club – and they should be as a matter of course – you could find yourself travelling the length and breadth of the country for a day out.

Clubs send out prospectuses freely and without question – obviously, to advertise their business – but are less open-handed with their accounts. I received about a dozen prospectuses while researching this section, but only one club responded positively to a request for a set of accounts. That is not to suggest that any-thing is amiss. They may simply have been unavailable, or new clubs may not yet have compiled them. However, it is a tack worth pursuing because they should outline possibly contentious areas such as directors' fees and any jockey retainers.

Both should be in keeping with the size of the club's oper-ations. A smaller club paying abnormally high fees to its directors may be suffering an unhealthy drain on its finances. Equally, where a club has taken a retainer on a jockey, it should have suffi-cient horses to justify the outlay, and the jockey should be worth the money. Paying a retainer to a rider who is not in constant demand is pointless. The club can probably get him anyway when required. If he has taken another ride, there will be plenty around of the same calibre.

Explore, too, the question of telephone tipping lines (often on the premium 0898 numbers) operated by the majority of clubs. It is a source of enormous revenue which keeps some clubs afloat, and you should be sure that the profits are returned to the club. British Thoroughbred Racing & Breeding, at its peak one of the country's most successful clubs, took, in one season, some £250,000 through their 'hotlines'. Despite substantial running costs, they were still able to plough about £80,000 back into the club. Keeping abreast of club news and the welfare of the horses, particularly those thought worth backing, is a large part of the thrill of membership. But, as the meter ticks over, the proceeds of your call should be bound for the club rather than a pocket some way removed from the members' best interests.

Racing clubs come in all shapes and sizes, some more success-ful than others. Provided you have satisfied yourself that your choice is competently organised and is likely at least to give you a run for your money, clubs can provide an excellent format for the owner, especially the newcomer. Certainly you may lose every penny of your investment, but at least you know exactly how much that could be.

It is an opportunity to savour a portion of racing's feast at limited cost and, if the experience proves sufficiently palatable, there is ample scope to return in other, more personal, forms of ownership.

Types of ownership

Although what are generally recognised as 'racing clubs' are limited companies, the Jockey Club allows for clubs in a different guise. Under the Rules of Racing, a club (for example, a tennis club) must have been established for a minimum of two years before applying for registration 'for normal social and recreational pursuits, and that those pursuits have not, and have never had, any connection direct or indirect with racehorse ownership anywhere in the world'. In those circumstances, the legal ownership of the horse is vested in four appointed trustees, each of whom must be a registered owner, on behalf of the club. The trustees are then responsible for the horse, which is entered by one of the trustees but runs in the name of the club and is also funded by the club. There is no standard application form, but a written application, including the rules of the club and a list of members, is required. Registration of a club is £75 plus VAT.

3: Buying a horse

Having decided which form of ownership will suit you best, the question of buying a horse is ready to be addressed. That is not quite correct – the aim is not simply to buy a horse, but to buy the right horse.

But how to unearth that successful horse? There are four basic methods of becoming a racehorse owner: by buying at a recognised bloodstock sales, by buying a horse already in a trainer's yard, through newspaper advertisements, and by securing a horse out of a selling or claiming race. With those broad options in mind, you will need to decide first upon a budget and then on what type of horse interests you most. Both are subjective issues. What you feel you can afford is entirely a personal matter, preference for the Flat or National Hunt racing only marginally less so.

If you fall into the Flat racing category, the chances are that you will be looking at two-year-olds. You can, of course, quite happily purchase older horses for the Flat but, by the time they are three-year-olds, their merit will have been established and many, particularly those running over middle distances, will have been targeted by the jumping owner to race over hurdles.

The National Hunt owner will be weighing up three-year-olds racing on the Flat with an eye first on hurdles, and perhaps looking further ahead to a steeplechasing career. The market in three-year-olds, particularly the better class horse, is often strong because of the appeal of the Daily Express Triumph Hurdle at the Cheltenham Festival in March. It is the championship for first-season hurdlers, by then four-year-olds, and a wonderful feather in the cap of the successful owner. It is invariably hotly-contested and the competition for suitable runners is as fierce as it can be expensive.

To buy a successful steeplechaser is hardest of all. Without paying big money for an already established chaser, the owner must base his purchase on potential, then exercise patience, and be prepared to accept no little expense as the horse develops. Perhaps only several years later will he know whether he has a chaser or not.

Owners looking at horses already running over hurdles or fences, or indeed established Flat racers, should be convinced that the object of their affections still has some scope for improvement. There is little point buying a horse which is badly handicapped, that is, has been given more weight than it really deserves, or is from a stable which may already have got the best out of it.

Trainers differ in the treatment of their horses. Some have a notoriously hard training regime designed to get to the bottom of a horse. Anything submitted by them at the sales is unlikely to have much more to offer. In contrast, others are especially sympathetic. Horses from their stables will be more attractive secondhand buys. Knowing who you are buying from is as important as knowing what you are buying for. Learn as much as you can about the methods of individual trainers. It is a fascinating study in itself and could also prove financially advantageous when applied to the bloodstock market.

At whatever level you enter the market, and through whichever avenue, always remember that bloodstock dealing is riddled with hazards, even for the experienced. It is no coincidence that describing someone who lives on his wits as 'a bit of a horse trader' has entered into common parlance. The business can be treacherous water inhabited by sharks all too ready to dine on the unwary.

Buying a horse

Buying at public auction

The bloodstock auction remains the most popular method of buying and selling horses. The rules are simple: the horse is led around the ring, bids are offered to the auctioneer and the highest, provided it exceeds any reserve (minimum selling price), secures the horse. The auctioneer will not disclose the reserve price, although it is usually made known if a horse is being offered without reserve.

Buyers are free to examine the horses, described as lots, beforehand. It is common practice to ask the vendor to bring the horse out of its box for a closer inspection, and to request a walk or trot up and down to examine its gait. One of the most frequent sights at any sale is of men wearing frowns of concentration as horse after horse is paraded before them. Mostly they are blood-stock agents – men, and nowadays an increasing number of women, who make their living buying horses on behalf of owners.

Bidding at auctions is not confined to agents, and is indeed free to anyone who has made themselves, and the extent of their credit, known to the sales company in advance.

The potential owner is perfectly entitled to bid on his own behalf. But before he puts that plan into action he should be sure he is sufficiently well-informed to know what he is doing. The thought of buying your own horse is undeniably attractive, but it can be a costly vanity.

If you feel safer relying on an agent but are uncertain how to go about contacting one, the best starting point is the Federation of Bloodstock Agents (GB) Ltd, based at Tetbury in Gloucester-shire. One of the most important aims of the Federation is to give the buyer confidence through employing an agent to help him in his purchase. *Caveat emptor* (let the buyer beware) is a maxim which should not be forgotten, but the federation can at least help get owners off on the right foot.

The federation will put you in touch with one or more of its members. It also publishes a booklet listing its members and will send a copy on request. Take several names and either write or telephone until you find one with whom you feel comfortable. Set out what you are looking for, what you hope to achieve

JOHN WARREN BLOODSTOCK

Among those purchased in the eight years
since its formation are the following
Black Type winners:–

Bought as yearlings

PARK EXPRESS
Gr.1 Cheveley Park Stakes

CREAG-AN-SGOR
Gr.1 Middle Park Stakes

MISTER MAJESTIC
Gr.1 Middle Park Stakes

MISS DEMURE
Gr.2 Lowther Stakes

JOVIAL
Gr.2 Cinema Stakes
Gr.2 Swaps Stakes

CONTRACT LAW
Gr.2 Richmond Stakes

MINATZIN
Gr.3 Prix de Conde

CAMEROUN
LR Goffs Silver Flash Stakes

Bought as Horses in Training

SALSE
Gr.1 Prix de la Foret

MOUNTAIN BEAR
Gr.1 Santa Barbara Stakes

SHORT SLEEVES
Gr.1 Ramona Stakes

DRUMALIS
Gr.2 Bay Meadows Stakes

THORNDOWN
LR San Jacquinto H'cap

Also
**LONGBOAT,
TOP SOCIALITE,
DOMINION ROYALE,**
Group Stallion **VIKING
FAMOUS STAR,
MORCON,** etc.

JOHN WARREN BLOODSTOCK

Hawstead Lodge, Hawstead, Bury St. Edmunds, Suffolk.
Tel: 0638 662401 or 0836 501777. Fax: 0638 666465.

and any general thoughts you may have. Although it is a specialist field, and one in which the newcomer is prone to feeling
overawed, do not be afraid to ask questions. Nor should you be
intimidated if your budget falls somewhat short of the Arabs'
armoury.

Any worthwhile agent will be prepared to listen. If he is not,
look elsewhere. Talk to different people, and, rather like attending interviews simply to practise the technique, you will learn a
little more from each one until you are ready to make a choice.
The first person you talk to is not necessarily the one with whom
you will end up doing business.

An agent's standard charge is 5 per cent of the purchase price.
For that, he will act as your guide through the maze. In truth,
racing is a small village in which most of the inhabitants are
known to each other. An agent spends his working life rubbing
shoulders with them and should know those with whom to do
business.

Once you have settled on an agent, he is likely to want to vet
you, particularly if you are a newcomer. He may require a
banker's reference to make sure you are creditworthy, and will
probably also ask for written confirmation of your instructions –
for example, that you wish to spend 20,000 guineas on a two-
year-old. Some agents still work on a basis of trust, but it is a
sobering fact of modern commercial life that a man's word is not
always his bond.

On the subject of money, he may well ask permission to keep a
couple of extra bids up his sleeve just in case. He may find a suitable individual which he feels is well worth perhaps a thousand
or two more, on the basis that if you have gone so far you might
as well go the rest of the way. That latitude is not a blank cheque.
It is simply recognising the fact that it is impossible to predict
exactly the sale price of a particular horse, and a good agent will
not use your goodwill as a bottomless purse. However, as a
double safeguard, you can always specify in writing an absolute
top limit. In our example, an agent would be instructed not to
exceed, say, 25,000 guineas, whatever the circumstances.

Most owners who visit the sales are more at risk from their own
extravagance than their agent's. Bloodstock auctions are exciting

and colourful events which set the adrenalin flowing, particularly for the uninitiated. Several agents have remarked on the phenomenon of being accompanied to the sales by a client who becomes so intoxicated by the atmosphere that accepting defeat becomes unthinkable. Egged on by the auctioneer's patter 'Don't lose this one now, sir', 'This is the one you've been waiting for' and the old faithful 'He's a bargain at this price', the client pushes his agent onward. Finally the horse is his, but for rather more than he intended. Go and enjoy the sales by all means, but keep a hold on reality in the face of temptation.

Written confirmation is as much for the agent's protection as for the owner's. Without it, an agent can quite easily be landed with a horse. It is not unknown for an owner to disappear into thin air, or for a supposed client to disown a horse as having cost more than agreed. A verbal agreement, as the film mogul Sam Goldwyn once reputedly observed, is not worth the paper it is written on.

Setting up the agent-client relationship takes time, and that, obvious though it may sound, is worth remembering. If you are thinking about owning a two-year-old, the major yearling sales take place in the autumn in Britain, mainly from September to November. You will therefore want your agent primed and ready to go by that time, so, unless you are on familiar enough terms to be able to give instructions at short notice, begin the search for a suitable candidate during the summer. Give yourself time to do a thorough job.

Once the relationship is in place, the agent can go to work. He will first want to establish the guidelines. Are you in it for business or pleasure? What type of horse do you want? How much are you prepared to spend?

If you have already made contact with a trainer, he may act in place of the agent, buying on your behalf. However, he is likely to charge the same fee, and many trainers also work in conjunction with agents. With trainers' workloads increasing, agents do much of the preparatory work for them, scouring the catalogues and liaising with the trainer on likely purchases.

Buying a horse
The sales circuit

For circuit, substitute circus. It moves from town to town and country to country, the regular performers always on parade, always in the thick of the action.

The acme of the bloodstock sales is the yearling market, those days of hope when every lot just could be a very good horse. Men pay exceedingly large amounts of money to discover the difference between reality and illusion. The yearling market in America and Europe reached its zenith towards the middle of the Eighties, borne upwards on the tide of Arab and international money. It took until 1982 before a million-guinea sale was achieved in Europe, when the three-year-old filly Tenea made 1,020,000 guineas. Yet less than a year later, that figure was bettered three times at the Tattersalls Highflyer sales. Those heady days became a memory as the market fell back to more realistic levels during the second half of the decade.

Breeding racehorses, as much as buying them, is a business of dreams. Breeders are spurred on by thoughts of producing a future Derby winner and, while that persists, there will always be plenty of yearlings from which to choose.

There are three main venues in Britain: Tattersalls in Newmarket, on the fringe of the town centre next to the railway station; Doncaster Bloodstock Sales, just across the road from the racecourse; and Ascot, also close to the course, down in a hollow a couple of hundred yards behind the main grandstand. That order – Newmarket, Doncaster and Ascot – reflects their overall status, although even within the three, individual sales vary considerably in importance. Tattersalls are also represented in Ireland at Fairyhouse, near Dublin, while Goffs, based at Kill in Co Kildare, has become increasingly influential.

Goffs is predominantly concerned with the sale of Flat horses. Through shrewd and aggressive marketing, they have assumed an ever higher profile, culminating in the Million Sale, inaugurated with the jewellers Cartier. Tattersalls' Irish operation deals primarily with National Hunt horses, although they are steadily building up the Flat side of the business.

Nor in these days of growing internationalism should overseas sales be forgotten. Deauville, on the Normandy coast of France,

If you are considering buying a racehorse, buy at the
TATTERSALLS/TIFFANY 1990
Highflyer Yearling Sales
OCTOBER 3rd - 5th

Buying a horse

has the bonus of sales being conducted in delightful surroundings. The North American arena is no longer the sole province of the sport's big spenders. The gathering of equine blue-bloods at Keeneland in Kentucky is best known to observers in Britain. Yearling sales in America begin in July, and, depending on the dollar rate, can be an attractive proposition.

For an owner prepared to spend upwards of £30,000, the American sales are an option worth serious consideration. The less fashionable sales still offer good quality horses, often in greater numbers than in Europe, simply because of the size of the industry. Allow around £3,000 transport costs back to Britain.

Buying abroad also has the attraction of favourable VAT treatment. Imported horses are not liable for VAT on the purchase price if shipped abroad again with two years. They do not have to be returned to the country of purchase. Thus, a horse purchased in America may be sent to Ireland. Also, should the horse prove to be talented, and therefore valuable, the owner has the option of paying the VAT to keep it in Britain.

Throughout the world, different sales attract different types of horses. Taking the British Isles, the Tattersalls Highflyer Sales are noted for classically-bred, high-priced yearlings. Goffs, too, is suited to the up-market individual, principally the Million Sale. The Doncaster St Leger Sales specialise in yearlings likely to make sharp two-year-olds.

For the National Hunt owner, the horses-in-training sales, common to all companies, is the probable first port of call. The reasons for sale vary considerably. Flat trainers often use the sales, especially those during the autumn, to clear out their stables and make room for the influx of yearlings. Some horses will be sold because they have not lived up to expectations. Others will be offered to settle a dispute between the owners.

Sometimes the reason for sale is obvious, sometimes rather less so. Always remember that a horse in training has been subjected to stresses which may have left a mark. It may have picked up bad habits, become soured mentally by bad handling, or simply have a physical problem which the vendor will attempt to camouflage.

A straight question to the vendor's team is not guaranteed to receive a straight answer. Some trainers will tell you the story behind the sale. Others can prove a good deal more evasive. If you ask the lad in charge why the horse is being sold, the chances are you will receive an 'I don't know, I'm just leading him up'. It is up to you, or your agent, to be sure you are not buying a pig in a poke.

For anyone looking for a young hurdler, it is worth asking your agent to keep an eye open for horses he may be able to purchase privately. Many agents are on the lookout for potential jumpers as early as spring, and if a deal can be concluded ahead of the sales season it may spare the horse some hard races on the Flat.

Horses, like humans, cannot go on indefinitely without a rest. If a horse can be given a break between his Flat and National Hunt campaigns, he will be in a better frame of mind and therefore more likely to reproduce his best form. Also, the vast majority of National Hunt horses are geldings, which means they have been castrated. If a horse is gelded during the summer, he has plenty of time to recover before going hurdling.

Another source of jumpers is the specific National Hunt sales. These deal in the more stoutly-bred jumping stock which take time to mature. Horses sold here often have their first taste of the racecourse in National Hunt flat races (bumpers) but are generally less popular with owners looking for instant action. Doncaster stages such sales in May and August, and Tattersalls' Derby Sale in Ireland also promotes young stock.

Although owners are likely to put personal preference, Flat or National Hunt, above thoughts of value, it is National Hunt racing which gives greater scope for buying a good horse, more especially higher up the scale. An owner with £50,000 to spend will not be anything out of the ordinary in the Flat hierarchy but he should be able to buy a very useful National Hunt performer at that price, without having to compete against a flotilla of million-guinea opponents.

A feature of the bloodstock market during the last few years has been a swing towards jump horses as owners have become disillusioned with their purchasing power on the Flat. The shift has increased prices for National Hunt stock but enough of the differential remains to suggest that the trend will continue.

Buying a horse
The catalogue

The catalogue is the first contact you will have with a particular sale. It is always prepared in advance to give potential purchasers the opportunity of assessing what is on offer. Availability of catalogues is usually advertised in the sporting press.

A catalogue describes the composition of the sale and, in the case of mixed sales, sets out on which day each category of horse is due to be sold. For example, in a three-day sale, the first day may deal with horses in training, the second with yearlings, and the third with breeding stock. Clearly, if you are concerned with one area only, you want to be there on the appropriate day.

It will confirm the dates of the sale and the starting time each day. Also, sprinkled through the catalogue will be approximate selling times for certain lot numbers as a guide to the speed at which the sale is expected to progress. These are for information only. Bloodstock sales generally move more slowly, rather than faster, than planned, but it is unwise to base your timetable on what is a notional schedule.

Unless you know beforehand that you will only be interested in a particular lot, read the catalogue with a view to short-listing those which catch your eye. They can then be scrutinised in the flesh on the day of the sale. Some will be physically unappealing, and so the list of possibles is gradually whittled down.

Be realistic in your initial assessments. A yearling by a successful sire out of a good-class mare is likely to fetch big money. The same applies to a talented Flat racer submitted at a horses-in-training sale. If you have a limited budget, there is no point passing your time at the sale with your nose pressed against the window of the store's most exclusive department.

The first pages of the catalogue are devoted to the conditions of sale. They describe the company's policy on various aspects of the sale, including bidding, payment, settlement of disputes and so on. Although the conditions are couched in the sort of legalese which never makes for easy reading, they are worth a few minutes' study, especially if you intend bidding on your own behalf. The sale will be conducted subject to the conditions, so if you do not know what is going on, the repercussions will be on your own head.

YEARLING, from Parsonage Farm Stud
the Property of Beaufort Bloodstock Ltd.

Will stand at Park Paddocks, Highflyer Paddock E, Box 47

About

113 (WITH VAT)

1.30

p.m.

A BAY FILLY
Foaled
April 8th, 1988

Thatching	Thatch (USA)	Forli (ARG)
		Thong
	Abella †	Abernant
		Darrica
La Melodie (1972)	Silly Season	Tom Fool
		Double Deal
	La Mome	Princely Gift
		La Parisienne

N.B.-Fillies Premium Form Signed.

1st Dam
LA MELODIE, placed once at 3 years;
dam of **six winners**-

EASTERN RED	(1977 f. by Forlorn River), won 1 race at 2 years and placed once.
MY ADRIANA	(1979 f. by Roman Warrior), won 1 race at 3 years and £1801 and placed twice.
Action Research	(1980 f. by Habat), unraced.
HARVARD	(1981 c. by Mansingh (USA)), won 1 race at 2 years and £7997, placed 3 times including fourth in Pacemaker Diomed Stakes, Epsom, **Gr.3**; also won 12 races in U.S.A., £38,744 including Q.Hollywood Park.
BAY PRESTO	(1982 g. by Bay Express), won 1 race at 2 years and £3745 and placed 3 times; also won 4 races in France, £5201; also placed once over jumps.
Conde d'Serafim	(1984 c. by Song), unraced.
Lagash	(1985 f. by Mansingh (USA)), won 6 races in Italy, £18,605, placed third in Premio Alessandro Perrone, Rome, **L.**
SIR RUFUS	(1986 c. by Thatching), won 1 race, £4013 at 2 years, 1988.

2nd Dam
LA MOME, won 3 races, £6053 at 2 and 3 years including Princess Elizabeth Stakes, Epsom;
dam of **four winners** viz-

LA LUTINE, won 4 races at 2 and 3 years and £8458 and placed once; dam of 2 winners viz-

    MON TRESOR, Champion 2yr old in Germany in 1988, 3 races at 2 years, 1988 and £64,712 including Tattersalls Middle Park Stakes, Newmarket, **Gr.1**, placed 3 times including third in Ladbroke European Free Handicap, Newmarket, **L.**; also won 1 race in Germany, £21,886 viz, Moet & Chandon Rennen, Baden-Baden, **Gr.2**.

    MONTENDRE, 2 races at 2 years, 1989 and £13,982 including Dewhurst Rockingham Stakes, York, **L.** and placed once.

LAMYA, 3 races in Sweden, £2075.

HOPEFUL HEIGHTS, won 2 races at 2 years and £9651 and placed 7 times; also placed twice over jumps.

MOMELLO, 1 race in Italy, £1049; also 2 races over jumps in Italy, £1354.

3rd Dam
LA PARISIENNE, **won** 2 races at 3 years and placed 7 times;
dam of **four winners** including-

    LA MOME, see above.

    LA HORSETTE (FR), 2 races in France; dam of 2 winners viz-
      PRINCE GRIS (FR), 5 races in France, 131,200 fr.
      PRINCE DANCING (FR), 4 races in France.

The next dam **LA BAILLE**, Champion 3-y-o filly in England in 1950, **won** 3 races at 3 years including Park Hill Stakes, Doncaster, Ribblesdale Stakes, Royal Ascot, placed second in Oxfordshire Stakes, Newbury, Cheshire Oaks, Chester and third in Newmarket Oaks and fourth in Oaks Stakes, Epsom; also **won** 1 race in France;
dam of **seven winners**-

La Bastille, unraced; dam of-

    BASTION, 1 race viz Coventry Stakes, Kempton Park.

    LA MIRABELLE, 1 race; dam of **JEROBOAM**, 3 races including Beeswing Stakes, Newcastle, **L.**; sire in Australia.

    LA COURONNE, 1 race; dam of **LA SOUVRONNE (NZ)**, 6 races including AJC Oaks, Randwick, **Gr.1**.

    La Bonne, unplaced; grandam of **BELLA NEGRA**, 5 races including Norsk Oaks, Ovrevoll, **Gr.1**.

*Page from a sales catalogue illustrating use of 'black-type'
(reproduced by courtesy of Tattersalls)*

Buying a horse

Without attempting to paraphrase the conditions, two are worth special attention. To quote from Tattersalls' catalogue: 'Purchasers are advised to inspect each lot prior to purchase. Each lot is sold as it stands and there is no term implied in any sale that the lot is of merchantable quality or is fit for training or any particular purpose'. Although I have borrowed Tattersalls' wording, the principle is universal. The onus is on the buyer to ascertain a horse's soundness and well-being.

There are circumstances in which horses bought at auction can be returned, but these are specific and are outlined in the conditions of sale.

The second is that the purchaser is responsible for the horse from the fall of the hammer. Anyone intending to buy and, again, this is especially true of people acting without a trainer or agent to guide them, should be aware that it is up to them to resolve the ensuing questions. The horse must have a home to go to, be it a training stable, stud farm or the purchaser's own property. It will need transport to take it there and insurance to cover the worst eventualities. Although transport and insurance firms are on hand at most major sales, forward planning will not go amiss.

Once you have laid the groundwork by reading the conditions of sale, you can move on to the greater pleasures of assessing the horses involved. Catalogues generally present only the first three generations of a horse's pedigree, but that should be more than sufficient to judge its likely merit and therefore selling price.

A yearling which has not yet been named is described by colour and sex – for example, a bay filly or a chestnut colt. Additionally with yearlings, the date of birth is given and, if it is the first foal, of its dam. Older horses offered for sale are identified simply by name and age. In bloodstock terminology, a male is a colt up to and including the age of four unless he has become a stallion (a horse which has taken up stud duties). From five and upwards, he is described as a horse. A female is a filly up to and including the age of four, unless she has been covered (mated), when she becomes a mare. Any female aged five or upwards is a mare regardless of her breeding activities. A gelding is a male horse which has been castrated, whatever its age.

Foaling dates of yearlings are worth a second look. On

1 January, a yearling automatically becomes a two-year-old regardless of when its birthday falls. It follows, then, that when two-year-olds begin to race, some are actually two years old and others are not. The thinking runs that those who are physically two will be more advanced than those who are not, and therefore more likely to reveal their ability early in their career. That argument applies principally to those considering sharp, early two-year-olds, because, as horses grow older, the difference becomes less pronounced until it disappears altogether.

The presentation of the immediate family tree concentrates on the racing and breeding records of the first three dams. The distaff, or female, line is annotated both in speech and the written word by the numbering of the dams. The mother of the horse in question is the first dam, usually referred to simply as the dam. Moving back in the pedigree, the grandmother, or grand-dam, is the second dam; the great-grandmother is the third dam; and fourth dam, fifth dam and so on, depending on how many more generations, or removes, are examined.

For easy reference, the racing ability of the mares can be judged by the system of 'black-type'. Mares are categorised as follows:

MARE Winner of a European Pattern race, a foreign graded stakes race, a listed race or a major American stakes race
Mare A horse placed in any of the above
MARE Winner of a flat race
Mare Winner of a National Hunt race or a non-winner
Mare Winner of a National Hunt Pattern race
Mare A horse placed in a National Hunt Pattern race

This example is taken from Tattersalls. Although it is specifically their style, it illustrates the different modes of presentation for different classes of horse. Each sales company has its own style. Be acquainted with the prevailing practice so that you are familiar with the manner in which pedigrees are presented.

The system is designed so that the most successful horses are the most eye-catching. Black-type applies to the mare's produce as well as to her own racing career. It is quite possible for a mare which never won to produce the winner of a Pattern race, enhancing her own value in the process.

Black-type is an important part of an owners' and trainers' thinking where fillies are concerned. When discussing future plans, trainers often say: 'We'll try and get some black-type into her pedigree', a recognition of its importance. To have black-type, especially as a winner, is a major selling point both for the filly herself and for her subsequent offspring. Little wonder that British trainers tend to send fillies across Europe in search of a soft touch. Indeed, in many cases the prize-money is secondary to the kudos of a Pattern race success. Italy, where competition is markedly less fierce than in Britain, France and Ireland, has become a popular venue for trainers attempting to increase the attractiveness of their charges.

There is an argument against the black-type system. The suggestion is that it devalues itself by a lack of discrimination. Pattern races are not of equal status – and nor are the horses which win them. The standing of one particular race can change fundamentally from year to year depending on the level of competition it attracts. The blanket black-type system suggests a winner of the same standard each time.

One possible remedy proposes that black-type horses be accompanied by their rating in the annual International Classifications, compiled by Europe's senior handicappers as a table of merit. It would then be possible to see precisely which are the best horses. The idea has attracted support within the industry, and, while the sales companies have yet to be persuaded to adopt it, the question is being considered.

Black-type horses are the icing on the cake of a pedigree. Some pedigrees, notably at the year's top sales, are peppered with high-class horses. Others, at the lower end of the scale, struggle to muster the odd one or two.

The pedigree shown in a catalogue usually shows the full breeding record of the dam, including those offspring which have not won races. The second and third dams feature a more selective offering of better-class winners. It will also include a brief resumé of the various dams' racing careers, mentioning by name any big events they may have won or been placed in.

As the pedigree is compiled on behalf of the vendor, usually by

a specialist company, winners will be recruited from all branches
of the family, no matter how remote their connection with the
individual being sold. Outright lies will not be tolerated but you
may not see all of the truth.

Pedigrees

The only certainty of pedigrees is that they will always confound
you. No animal species is better documented than the Thoroughbred, yet, after more than two centuries of controlled racing and
breeding, the laws of reproduction decree that luck will always
be a major factor.

The history of the Thoroughbred goes back to three Oriental
stallions imported into England during the 17th and 18th centuries. Every modern Thoroughbred traces its ancestry in the
male line to The Byerley Turk (imported 1689), the Darley
Arabian (circa 1704), or The Godolphin Arabian (1730). Mating
with the more robust native English mares gradually developed
what we know today as the Thoroughbred.

Interpreting a pedigree, and attempting to gauge a horse's
prospects, is a fascinating exercise, but one in which chance
ultimately plays a big part in getting the right answer. The
breeders' old saying 'Send the best to the best and hope for the
best' remains the watchword.

The first decision in a pedigree is taken by the breeder selecting which stallion should cover his mare. As everywhere else in
racing, fashion plays its part. A stallion's status is governed by the
success of his offspring, which in turn controls how well his
future crops will sell (a critical consideration for a commercial
breeder) and therefore decides the fee at which a stallion stands.
The more successful the stallion, the higher the fee.

The breeder's problem is that he must work three years in
advance. During the autumn of 1990, he will decide his matings
for 1991. The mare will foal in 1992 and it will be the end of 1993
before the yearlings are sold. Three years can be an eternity in the
working life of a stallion. He may have been a star in 1990, but
three lean seasons can swiftly put him back in the chorus. It can,
of course, work in reverse. A breeder may take a risk with an
unfashionable stallion only to see the value of his stock soar in

the interim. The gamble is considerable.

Having set up the mating to the best of his ability, the breeder is in the lap of the Gods. It is a law of genetics that the foal will inherit 50 per cent of its genes from the sire and 50 per cent from the dam, and no amount of agonising over the covering will change that. However, with that in mind, some stallions and mares seem more capable of transmitting favourable traits than others. When you assess pedigrees, a basic rule is to sift out proven performers. You will be taking a chance with a stallion which has done little in several years at stud. Equally a mare which has produced six losers from six foals is a bad bet to hit the jackpot next time.

Inevitably there are exceptions. Given the unpredictability of genetics, it could hardly be otherwise. You only have to look at your friends. How many brothers and sisters do you know who bear little resemblance to each other? Each season produces horses which have beaten all the odds to win races, overcoming plebeian breeding to eclipse better-bred and more expensive rivals. But they are exceptions, a minority among the great mass of unfashionably-bred horses which reliably live down to expectations.

One rule-of-thumb generally applied to pedigrees, with particular reference to two-year-olds, is that the racing and breeding records of the sire is a fair guide to their distance requirements and precocity. Mummy's Pet, a high-class sprinter who included three two-year-old wins in his six career victories, transmitted those characteristics of speed and early development to much of his stock. His stud career was notable for the production of sprinters and sharp juveniles.

In contrast, a middle-distance performer, such as the 1974 St Leger winner Bustino, is likely to be better known for siring horses which improve as they tackle longer distances. Many of them will improve at three on what they achieved at two. Sires in this category do have juvenile winners but mostly in the second half of the season when the youngsters run over 7 furlongs and beyond.

Unfortunately, stayers are the kiss of death commercially nowadays. Staying races have declined in popularity (more with owners and trainers than the racegoing public it should be said), so staying-bred horses are at a low ebb.

Although the dam will clearly play a part, perhaps adding stamina in a mating with a sprinter or injecting speed to counteract a stayer, it is generally fair comment that anyone looking for an early sort should concentrate on sprinting sires, or those with a proven record of early two-year-olds.

The pedigree is only half of the equation when it comes to assessing horses. Nor is it necessarily the more important half. Conformation is at least equally vital. If the horse has a physical shortcoming, it may not be able to produce its best on the racecourse, regardless of how well bred it may be.

Having 'an eye for a horse' is a talent learned only by many hours studying the horse's physical make-up, if it is learned at all. The brilliant Irish trainer Vincent O'Brien, who has done more than anybody to establish the immensely-successful Northern Dancer sire-line in Europe, would spend hours gazing at yearlings, imagining how they would look as they matured. His record in the world's great races speaks for itself.

The skill in judging a horse's conformation is not only in recognising the faults, but in knowing how significant they could be to racing capability. There are very few text-book horses around. Lord Derby's Hyperion, the 1933 Derby winner, is held by many to have been the 'perfect' horse, yet even he was noticeably small at not much more than 15 hands.

One agent tells of his regular visits to watch horses in the winner's enclosure: 'You see a horse after he has won and you ask yourself: Would I have bought him? The answer is probably no. But the more you see horses and the more experienced you become, the more you learn to accept certain flaws. In the end you know what you can get away with.' Most bloodstock buyers tend to concentrate on the horse's walk, eye, legs and his scope for maturing. Trying to put a visual art into words is all but impossible. If you believe you have a feel for it, ask yourself: Do you recognise the condition of horses in the paddock on racedays?

If so, test the water by attending a few bloodstock sales before you are tempted to buy, just to get the feel of looking at the lots on offer. If, however, you do not have it, there is nothing to worry about. Professional help is always at hand.

Colt or filly?

This discussion applies primarily to those owners considering two-year-olds. To buy an older horse suggests a decision on its future has already been taken. Colts from the Flat are likely to go jumping; fillies will probably be bought with a view to breeding in the not too distant future.

Many buyers in the two-year-old market give little thought to the value of their purchase in the long-term. Buoyed by dreams of greatness, they think no further than their youngster winning races. The cold fact that the vast majority fail to do so should not be overlooked. If your horse is among them, where do you go then?

It has always been fashionable to buy colts, particularly in the higher reaches of the market. The reason is clear: if you buy a million-guinea yearling, the only way to make the investment pay is to create a stallion. High-priced colts are bought not simply for their racecourse potential, but with an eye to stud fees should they prove top-class runners on the track. Colts offer the possibility of the jackpot, fillies much less so.

A successful stallion will cover around 45 mares each season at a conservative estimate, generating a minimum of 45 times his not inconsiderable stud fee. A filly, or mare as she is described once at stud, can have only one foal each year (twins are much disliked by the breeding industry). Even the produce of an outstanding mare and a high-class stallion will only rarely fetch anything like what a stallion will bring in fees. The arithmetic, then, all points towards the desirability of colts.

That scenario describes the top of the market. But only the privileged few inhabit those upper echelons, and what holds good for them may not necessarily be the best policy for everybody. Clearly, anyone who buys a colt has the chance of finding that pot of gold, as anyone who does the football pools may one day land the big pay-off. However, there is a yawning gulf between possibility and probability.

If, by the middle of his three-year-old career, your colt has

43

shown almost no trace of ability, he is all but worthless. He may improve over hurdles to pick up a couple of races, but is that likely? More to the point, would any buyer be willing to pay to find out?

Fillies do, however, have some residual value. If you set out with the idea of buying a filly with a reasonable pedigree, ideally with some winners in the family to catch the eye of purchasers later on, and she shows some ability, she will always have something to offer as a broodmare. The question of pedigree is important, though. A filly with no worthwhile background is just as meagre an investment as a colt with no form.

An additional incentive is the Fillies' Premium Scheme. Broadly, fillies foaled or reared in Britain are eligible. The breeder and the owner co-sign the application for the scheme, which is then forwarded to Weatherbys. The cost of application, payable by the owner, is £35 plus VAT if the filly is registered before 28 February of the year in which she is a two-year-old, or £110 plus VAT after that date.

Once registered, fillies qualify for a possible share in a fund which will total £511,000 in the 1990 Flat season. It is administered by the Levy Board. A 40 per cent premium, based on guaranteed prize-money, will be paid to those qualifiers winning races confined to fillies. In Pattern races confined to fillies, the premium is 35 per cent, the winner taking 24.5 per cent, the second 7 per cent and the third 3.5 per cent. Races covered by the scheme, which includes claiming races but not sellers, are denoted in the annual Programme Book or the forthcoming races section of the *Racing Calendar* by the legend **FP**.

It does, however, seem to be something of a Cinderella set-up. In its promotional material, the Thoroughbred Breeders' Association (TBA), which represents the interests of British breeders, remarks that some breeders have not registered fillies which are eligible. It is a sad comment on the marketing of the scheme if the breeders themselves have failed to get the message. What hope can owners have of knowing that their newly-acquired yearling filly could qualify for extra prize-money? The final statistics for the 1989 scheme confirm those misgivings. Out of 303 races, only 124 of the premiums offered were won. In terms of hard cash, that represents just £262,000 from an allocation of £479,000.

A footnote to the figures is illuminating: 63 per cent of the premiums offered went to owner-bred fillies, a near two to one majority over those fillies which were bought. Clearly there is a lack of communication somewhere. The figures suggest that owners who buy fillies are either unaware of the scheme, or simply cannot be bothered to register. If the latter is the case, they should be bothered, and quickly, because for the sake of around £40 an excellent source of possible extra revenue is being ignored. The former is more probable. Greater contact between the breeder and the purchaser should be encouraged, ideally under the auspices of the TBA. The TBA should also take a more active role in advising owners, particularly newcomers, on the implications of the scheme.

Fillies and mares, regardless of age, also receive 5lb from colts and horses in all but Pattern races on the Flat. There is a uniform 5lb allowance in National Hunt racing.

This is not a campaign for blindly buying fillies. It is rather an attempt to redress what sometimes resembles a prejudice against them. There are undoubtedly points in their favour, and they are well worth thinking about before the final decision is made.

Buying from a trainer

Most trainers have horses ready to pass on. They are usually young stock, two-year-olds for the Flat or novice hurdlers over jumps, bought 'on spec' by the trainer with an eye to finding an owner later. That the trainer has bought the horses in the first place is an indication that he has faith in their potential. He has seen something in them, and has wanted them in his stable even if he does not have an owner in mind. This is where you come in.

Having bought the horses, clearly the trainer is keen to find an owner as soon as possible. Every day that they are in his name costs him money. He has paid for them out of his own pocket, or more probably his bank manager's, and has to keep them at his expense. The sooner he can find someone to relieve the burden, the better.

The trainer therefore has a pressing financial motive in

persuading you that here is, indeed, just the horse you have been looking for. Wearing his salesman's hat, he will present an enticing case. Do not be surprised to hear that you are admiring the most handsome colt in the stable, or the best-bred filly! Of course, you may be doing exactly that, but it pays to keep a sense of perspective. You would not immediately believe everything an estate agent or a car dealer told you, so hang on to that degree of scepticism. Buying a racehorse is much more an affair of the heart but the same business principles apply.

However, we may be getting ahead of ourselves. Before you can buy the horse, you need to find the trainer. The same rules apply to selecting a trainer here as in any other circumstances. Meet different people before settling on one; be clear of your own objectives in ownership; find someone you feel you will get on with. In fact, those rules count more than ever here. If you have already bought a horse, a significant step has already been taken. The horse's future will depend on your chosen trainer, but you have at least provided the raw material. In buying a horse from a trainer, you are making the two decisions simultaneously. If you pick the wrong trainer, you may well have the wrong horse as well.

It is naive to say that trainers will not sell you a bad horse. The great majority act honourably and will try to get you involved in what they believe to be the right horse. That is the sensible way for anyone taking the long-term view. If you are happy with this horse, you will probably stay with the trainer in future. The trainer has his own interests to protect.

Unhappily, not everybody subscribes to that notion. Some trainers have horses on their hands and are not overly concerned how they farm them out, as long as someone is paying the bills. The danger is greatest for the newcomer, who in his enthusiasm and innocence can be drawn into a bad buy.

One owner tells of being approached by a trainer offering him a horse which, the owner was assured, would land a gamble in a seller in three months' time. The owner declined. It proved to be a wise move, for not only did the horse not win, it never ran.

Existing owners will have had some experience of trainers. If they are happy with someone, they will continue to patronise him. If they choose to move on, they at least have some idea of what to look for next time. The first-time owner does not have that experience to draw upon. The best reference a trainer can have is word of mouth recommendation. If a friend gives a particular trainer a glowing report, he is clearly one to put on your short-list. Otherwise, a bloodstock agent may be able to help. Agents are in regular contact with trainers and will be aware of who has horses available.

Trainers may also be prepared to sell shares, probably a minimum of a quarter, in the horse. If you are looking at this possibility, be extremely careful when it comes to signing up for a partnership. Meet your partners if they were not previously known to you and satisfy yourself they are the right people to be doing business with. Remember, if they default, you, and the remaining partner(s), will be liable for their share.

The message, though, is always the same: do your homework, talk to people, know your aims. You will at least give yourself every chance of making the right decision.

Buying from newspaper advertisements
Many of the greatest dangers inherent in buying a racehorse gather here in the biggest minefield of all. There are imponderables everywhere. You could be buying from someone you have never heard of, assuming the advertisement even carries a name. Many give just a telephone number and some brief but alluring details: 'half-brother to four winners', 'sister to high-class two-year-old', 'to stay with top trainer' and so on. Everything must be investigated. Who were the winners? What and where did they win? Who says the two-year-old was high-class? Is the trainer really at the top of his profession? Nothing can be taken for granted. And never, ever, send money before you have seen the horse.

Some years ago, a prospective owner, impressed by a newspaper advertisement for a horse, sent cash to the address provided. By chance, his job as a lorry driver took him by the address soon afterwards, but as he went past he was horrified to see that it was an abandoned house. His 'trainer' had gone, and the money with him.

If an advertisement irresistibly takes your fancy, make thorough enquiries about your intended bedfellows. Ask for names and addresses, and make contact with them before committing yourself. It is an astonishing fact of racehorse ownership that people often enter into it with alarmingly little research. Buying a house or a car is certain to launch an armada of questions, yet a horse, also a major expenditure, can be purchased almost without a second thought.

Remember that any horse purchased privately should be examined for soundness prior to payment. If you are taking along your cheque book, take a vet as well.

Newspaper advertisements are by no means a platform for unbridled chicanery – owner Willie Braid paid a reputed six-figure sum for Joint Sovereignty to run in the 1990 Grand National after seeing an advertisement in *The Sporting Life* – but they do require as much vigilance as the potential owner can muster.

Buying out of a seller or claimer

This is the ultimate for owners seeking instant action. By either buying from a seller or claiming a horse, you immediately acquire a ready-made runner.

In the hierarchy of races, claimers and sellers are very much at the bottom of the league, with claimers being the better class of the two. That is the drawback of buying a horse in this way. You know exactly the type of horse you are going to get, and, frankly, it will not be very good.

Some selling winners do slip through the net. Jamarj, a good-class three-year-old of 1988, failed to attract a bid after winning a seller as a two-year-old. Next time, however, buyers were wise to her potential and connections had to pay 19,000 guineas to retain her after she landed another seller. Cats Eyes was bought for 3,400 guineas after winning a selling hurdle at Devon and went on to notch a string of successes in better class. They are, however, exceptions.

Most courses stage selling races, or selling plates as they are sometimes known (a horse which is considered selling race standard is often referred to as a plater). The quality varies from track to track: York and Newmarket, two of the country's leading courses, stage valuable sellers. Indeed, the standard of those races is above many non-selling races at smaller venues.

To buy a horse out of a competitive seller will cost a good deal more than buying out of a weak race. Think in terms of a five-figure sum to secure the winner of a valuable seller. At the bottom of the scale, horses go for a couple of thousand guineas. But that, too, is far from cast-iron. Bali Sunset, after winning a moderate seller on the Flat at Leicester in 1989, was bought in for 23,000 guineas.

The minimum selling price of the winner is equal to the added prize-money of the race. If the auctioneer cannot attract a bid at that price, he will announce 'No bid', and the horse will be retained by its owner. However, if bidders join battle, the auction will be conducted along established lines with the highest bid winning.

It is common for an owner to try to buy back his horse after it has won. If he succeeds, and it can be a costly victory should several others show interest, then the auctioneer will announce 'Bought in'. For owners, the economics of selling races virtually demand that the winner has been well backed by connections. Prize-money for this category of race is especially small, so it can quite easily cost considerably more to buy back the horse than it has actually won. The difference has to be made up by betting.

If this avenue to ownership appeals, make sure that you have sorted out the details beforehand. Once the horse is sold, it becomes your property immediately. You must have a trainer to send it to, and transport on hand to get it there. It is best to work with your trainer.

Beaten horses may also be claimed out of sellers, the minimum claiming price being advertised in the race conditions. Claiming races (or 'claimers') differ from sellers in that the winner is not automatically offered for sale. The premise of a claimer is that a horse is entered to be claimed for not less than the figure laid down by the race conditions, say, 10,000 guineas.

If an owner, or more usually the trainer if he is handling the entries, is happy to risk a horse being claimed for less than the 10,000 guineas in our example, that horse will receive a weight allowance which increases as the claiming price falls. The race conditions will then go on to specify that allowance – say, 1lb for every 500 guineas below the maximum claiming price. An owner, believing that 7,000 guineas is a realistic assessment of his horse's value, will enter it at that price. That puts him 3,000 guineas below the maximum, so his horse will be allowed to carry 6lb (1lb for each 500 guineas, as per the conditions) less than the top weight. The claiming price is usually displayed next to the horse on the official racecard bought at the course.

Once the race has been run, written claims must be submitted to the Clerk of the Scales within a set time after the race. The highest claim is successful. If two or more are submitted at the same price, the Clerk of the Scales will decide by ballot.

It is not unusual to see some odd figures offered as claims. For instance, if you are banking on being the only claimant, you could, following the example, offer 10,000 guineas. But if you feel someone else may be pursuing the same theory, you could put in 10,001 guineas. As with buying out of a seller, once a successful claim has been lodged the horse becomes your property. Make the necessary arrangements beforehand.

Unfortunately, claiming horses carries a rather unpleasant stigma. Many trainers regard having a horse claimed as barely removed from having it stolen, and are sometimes apt to greet the loss of the horse with particularly bad grace. That, however, is literally the name of the game. Claiming races are founded on horses being eligible to be claimed, and that is precisely what may happen. If, as an owner, you do not want to lose the horse, avoid running it in sellers or claimers.

Whichever method of buying a horse you eventually adopt, there is no guarantee of success. You can assemble the finest team of experts, pore over every catalogue and draw upon the fattest cheque book, but in the end you will need more than your share of good fortune to come up with a successful horse. Some owners can do nothing wrong, almost camping in the winner's enclosure as they welcome victory after victory. Others struggle for 20 years with barely a whiff of triumph. If, even after detailed preparation, things fail to go exactly to plan, it does not automatically mean someone was at fault. Luck is the most vital weapon in the owner's armoury: all you can do is try to keep its influence to a minimum.

4: Trainers

Although buying a horse and choosing a trainer are treated as separate decisions, they are closely related. Once you have settled on a particular type of horse, the field of likely trainers is automatically narrowed. If you have bought a sharp two-year-old with an eye to picking up some early-season races, there is little sense sending it to a trainer who is known for giving his juveniles plenty of time.

Equally, if you have a horse which will require plenty of time, it may be better to avoid a trainer renowned for getting his runners on the track as soon as possible. That is not to say that trainers are incapable of adapting to certain types of horses, nor that one man's *modus operandi* is necessarily superior to another's. Good trainers are sufficiently flexible to accommodate whatever needs are required, but many do have very personal styles. It is simpler for you to match the horse with the trainer which will best suit it, rather than expect the trainer to prepare it in a manner which may go against the grain.

Combining horse and trainer is only half the battle. There is also the question of matching owner and trainer. That can only be achieved by a clear assessment of your own motives. If you are a wealthy man in racing for business, the leading trainers are the answer. The same people are always in the news when the big

51

races come around, and it is they who have the proven ability and experience to take the top prizes. If you are in it for fun, a trainer with a smaller operation will be more suitable. He is likely to have more time to build a personal relationship with his owners and, if you do happen to have a good horse, you become much more of a big wheel in the stable. In a big yard, the merely good horse is commonplace and may be overshadowed by top-notchers bound for the Classics.

Trainers' attitudes are also important, but more difficult to define. There is the story of the couple who sent the apple of their eye to a trainer, only to be told several months later that it was quite useless. They were mortified that the family pet could be dismissed so ruthlessly. In contrast, a London businessman had several horses with a notably amenable and optimistic trainer. The owner was regularly assured that the horses were better than they had shown so far, were improving and that their day was not far away. By the end of the season, the result was the same. No wins and little to show for the investment. The businessman was furious and took his horses away.

The moral of such stories is that different owners want different shades of the truth. The couple would have liked a word of encouragement now and again, to have had the pill sugar-coated. The businessman, used to dealing with hard and often unpleasant facts, wanted the truth without any embellishments. Both were with the wrong trainer. None of the parties involved was at fault, they were simply ill-matched.

If you have bought your horse through an agent, he will be well placed to offer some insights into the way particular trainers' minds work. Should you be placing the horse yourself, tell the prospective trainer what you are looking for from the game. If you want the facts straight, make sure he is under no illusions.

A trainer once commented that the best news an owner can hear, other than being told he has a good horse, is that he has a bad one. Only the most sentimental owner wants to tolerate an all but worthless animal bleeding his funds. It is crucial to know the truth. All you can do is smile ruefully and get rid of it. A cardinal rule of racehorse ownership is to know when to cut your losses.

52

Trainers

If your trainer says your horse will never win a race, believe him. Racing is full of owners so besotted with their horses that they are blind to the truth. One owner, having been assured by her trainer that the animal in question could hardly get out of its own way, was so angered she immediately sent the horse to another trainer. Of course it has some ability, she thought, it just needs more sympathy. A growing list of trainers and thousands of pounds later, the awful truth, that the horse did indeed have nothing to recommend it, finally and painfully registered.   ·

One of racing's enduring arguments is the north versus south battle, which rages most intensely when trainers, and training fees, are under discussion. The major owners and trainers congregate around Newmarket and Lambourn, the country's two most important training centres. Thousands of winners are despatched from each every year, and, while no-one would denigrate either area, there is much to be said for looking carefully at trainers based elsewhere.

In an overwhelming number of cases, fees will be markedly lower. It is impractical to attempt to list the charges of individual trainers, even if they could be persuaded to reveal their fees. Some are notably reticent to talk where money is concerned, perhaps fearing that if owners can find another man a couple of pounds cheaper then the horses will be switched. That is short-sighted. Any trainer you approach, even without the promise of sending him a horse, should be happy to discuss his charges and what you will get for your money. Training racehorses is a business no less than any other. The customer, in this case the owner, should be presented with the choices available to him, then allowed to make his decision.

The north, certainly in recent years, has rarely attracted its due rewards in terms of good horses. That is no reflection on the quality of its trainers. Many northern trainers are the equal of their southern counterparts, and have wasted no time proving the fact when given the opportunity.

Clearly there is considerable status in having a horse trained at Newmarket or Lambourn. Remember though, it is a status which has its price. Not only in training fees, but in transport costs. Newmarket, especially, is not central to any of the Flat tracks except its own racecourse and perhaps Yarmouth, on the Norfolk coast. There is a conglomeration of courses in Yorkshire, with those further north and in Scotland readily accessible. That becomes an important consideration when the time comes for your horse to run. Transport is expensive – £1 per mile is generally reckoned to be a fair estimate – so if your Newmarket-trained horse has to travel to, say, Ripon in Yorkshire for its best opportunity, expect a substantial bill, even if the horse shares a box with other runners at the same meeting.

It is more sensible to think in reverse. If your horse is trained in the north, you are likely to have a series of suitable races much closer to home. Should your horse turn out to be useful, it then becomes worthwhile to consider sending it for a suitable race in the south.

Be practical. It would be wonderful if your horse turned out to be a world-beater, but that is closer to fantasy than reality. Regularly taking on the big boys at Sandown, Ascot, Goodwood and the like can be a disheartening experience when your horse is not good enough. Before long it may be journeying to one of the smaller northern tracks anyway, to give it a better chance of winning.

When it comes to National Hunt racing, there is probably even more scope. Lambourn dominates the jumping scene, as Newmarket does the Flat, but again it is folly to believe that the story ends there. Accomplished National Hunt trainers are dotted throughout the land, from Scotland to the West Country. Many jump trainers also have farming interests, so it is quite possible that their charges can be especially reasonable if they are growing their own feedstuffs.

This is not a plea for the small man at the expense of the high-powered trainers, nor an exercise in setting one area at the throat of another. There are good, bad and indifferent trainers at all levels of the sport and in all sorts of places. But do not fall into the trap of thinking that household names are imperative to successful ownership. Look beyond the obvious. With a little delving you can find a trainer on the same wavelength as yourself, perhaps at less than you thought.

The best way to whittle down the list is to visit trainers in their respective stables. Not only will you meet the trainer on his home ground, there is much to be gleaned from a look at the stables. Are they smart and well maintained or is paint peeling off everywhere? Does the yard smack of efficiency and sense of purpose? Do the staff appear cheerful? Pitchforks and wheelbarrows lying around do nothing for the general air of tidiness. Horses should be standing on clean bedding, and the boxes should be light and well-ventilated to cut down the risk of infection.

Much of this is intuitive. Some places just feel right, others do not. As you visit more stables, you will build up a picture in your mind of just what it is you are looking for. When you meet the trainer, take the opportunity to tackle him on some basic points.

Where does he run his horses? Some trainers are apparently hypnotised by the big meetings and always run horses there whether they have a chance of winning or not. If you want to be seen out and about, that may suit you. Other trainers run horses where they have the best chance regardless of how unfashionable the venue may be. If you do not mind going to some of the country's less glorious outposts, provided you have some prospects of success, then you should find a trainer with the same philosophy.

How many horses does each lad 'do'? Quality and quantity do not go hand-in-hand. Three is a fair answer, and any lad being asked to do more than that will inevitably have less time and attention to devote to each individual. Does the trainer employ a stable jockey? The advantage of a stable jockey is that he will ride horses at home and therefore have a better idea of how to handle them during races. On the debit side, stable jockeys are paid a retainer, which is usually an additional cost for the owner. The advantage is not something that comes free. It is also worth asking just how much say you or your partners will have in who rides your horse. Trainers can be fiercely protective of their favourite riders, sometimes to the point of telling an owner that if he does not like a particular jockey riding his horse he can take the horse away. You will be paying the bills, so find out where you stand.

55

Training licences

There are three categories of training licence: one by which a trainer may run only hurdlers or steeplechasers; one applying only to runners on the Flat; and a dual-purpose licence which covers both codes. Additionally, there is a large collection of 'permit holders', who are allowed to run horses under National Hunt rules either for themselves or for their immediate family.

The Flat-only licence is a rarity. Even the most Flat-orientated trainers usually have a dual-licence. Some have one or two jumpers to keep the yard ticking over during the winter, although the luckier ones find the occasional high-class jumper in the stable. In 1990, Michael Stoute and Barry Hills, both Classic-winning trainers on the Flat, fought out the finish of the Champion Hurdle with Kribensis and Nomadic Way respectively.

The majority of National Hunt trainers also prefer a dual-purpose licence. Many like to give their hurdlers a run on the Flat to sharpen them up for a forthcoming jumping campaign. There is also the possibility of picking up some prize-money on the level before their real business begins.

At any one time there are around 900 training licences current. A sample taken in February 1990 showed 370 dual licences, 366 permits, 104 jump-only licences and 22 Flat-only. Trainers and permit holders must satisfy the licensing committee of the Jockey Club of their suitability. Existing trainers are generally re-licensed each year without any trouble, but a new applicant must convince the committee, at an interview, of his experience of working with horses and that his premises and facilities meet the necessary standards.

On the score of experience, the two best-trodden avenues are to have worked previously as an assistant to an existing trainer, or be a former jockey. For an applicant to be granted a licence, he must also show that he has the requisite number of horses in his yard. For restricted licences, that is, Flat or National Hunt only, a trainer must have a minimum of 9 horses. For a dual-purpose licence he must have 12.

The Jockey Club also likes to see a spread of owners in the stable, rather than have the horses concentrated in two or three names. The more owners a trainer has, the greater is the demand for his services, and therefore the more likely he is to be granted a licence. Should the number of horses in the yard drop below the minimum levels, a trainer does not automatically lose his licence. The Jockey Club works on an annual basis, reviewing the numbers over a full year rather than relying on small, and perhaps unrepresentative, samples.

A National Hunt trainer will have fewer horses in the yard during the summer but may easily increase his string once the season starts in earnest. In another case, a trainer may have the misfortune to have several horses killed in quick succession, again taking him below the quota. The Jockey Club is, however, likely to discuss the renewal of a licence with a trainer should he consistently struggle to fill his boxes.

Similar principles apply to permit holders. There must be proof of experience before a licence is granted. Again, applicants may have worked with horses in some practical capacity, or have had some success training point-to-pointers before deciding to try to move up the scale.

There have been suggestions that the issuing of training licences be supported by the more formal assessment of competence favoured by other countries. In the United States, for example, many racing authorities run 'trainer testing' programmes, whereby the aspiring trainer is asked to pass both practical and written examinations before he is allowed to take up his chosen profession. The outcome of the test is not a foregone conclusion. In some areas, the pass rate is little better than 50 per cent. One would-be trainer, on being asked what he understood by the term 'gravel', replied that it was something used to maintain order at meetings.

Although it is easy to poke fun at some of the less accomplished applicants, the test is not designed specifically to sift out eccentrics. It imposes an overall standard, and if a racing state requires that the test be taken, then that means everyone. Even the legendary jockey Bill Shoemaker, who rode the best part of 9,000 winners in a career spanning more than 40 years, had to take the examination just like any other hopeful.

Of course, the Jockey Club does not hand out licences just because somebody asks for one. Yet the care of racehorses, and coping with the demands of owners, is an intricate and demanding field which will not become any easier.

The training regime

No two trainers prepare their horses in exactly the same way. If there were a text-book to be followed it would be easy, and training racehorses is anything but that. The only proof lies in the results. Winners are the sole arbiter of whether someone has it right or wrong.

Flat

For the Flat trainer, his first direct contact with a horse will be when it arrives as a yearling. Nowadays the yearlings bought at auction are generally used to being handled, particularly those prepared to look their best by commercial studs.

Trainers prefer to keep the yearlings out of the stable until the end of the season to minimise the risk of infection to those already in the yard. The majority of yearling sales take place in September and October, while the Flat season is still in progress, and trainers do not want the last months of the year wrecked by a bug carried in by one of the yearlings. Yearlings enter the stable towards the end of November. Some trainers break the yearlings themselves, that is, get them used to wearing tack and finally ready to be ridden. Others send their yearlings to people who specialise in breaking yearlings. Either way the result is the same.

With the yearlings in the yard, the trainer will begin to canter them steadily before Christmas. The yearling must learn to canter straight, then canter behind one of the older horses and go upsides other horses. Everything is new to him. He has to adjust to the strange sights and sounds of stable life, and the close proximity of other horses.

In the New Year, when yearlings become two-year-olds, work will be increased. As the pace is stepped up through January and February, the trainer will begin to assess which are likely to be the early types for the approaching turf season, and which will require more time. The two-year-olds will also be introduced to starting stalls, which will become a staple of their working lives.

In deciding whether a horse will be forward, a trainer will be governed by its breeding, its shape and size, and what kind of 'feel' it is giving its lad. Having marked a horse down as an early sort, the trainer will continue to increase its work until it is set to run. Most trainers err on the side of being easy on young horses. If they are over-cooked at the start of their careers, they may be ruined for life. If the trainer has been too easy, at least he still has the horse in one piece for another day.

Once the horse has run, it is generally given an easy few days before being brought back to racing pitch for its next outing. The process is repeated by the trainer throughout the season, on an ever-growing scale, as those horses which were given more time come into full training.

The basic principles apply to all age groups. Once the horse is fit, it should need only to be kept ticking over, unless it is injured during the year and need a rest to aid recovery. There should be a lesser element of the unknown with the older horses, though. They will already have had at least one season in training (unless they were unable to run because of injury or being backward), so there should be some clear hints about their strong points: whether they are sprinters or stayers; if they go well early on or need a run to put them just right; if they are happier on firm or soft ground; and so on. A trainer will also try to give a horse a rest during the season to keep him fresh.

The training regime can be determined by the weather. A prolonged dry spell will make the ground too firm to risk horses. Although its effects are most obvious on race fields, which are greatly reduced, there is a concurrent effect on training. Even when the weather breaks again, it takes time to bring the horses back to peak fitness as the rain eases the training grounds.

Stable life begins early. Groups of horses are described as lots, and the first lot will pull out around 7.00 am. Second and third lots will follow at 9.30 am and just after 11.00 am. When the last of the horses have returned, the yard is swept and left quiet by midday to give the horses some peace and quiet to get over their work.

Evening stables is between four and five, when the trainer will make an inspection tour of the horses, though not necessarily all of them every day. He will look to make sure the horse has eaten up properly (always a good sign) and check with the lad that the horse has suffered no ill-effects from either racing or recent work.

National Hunt

National Hunt racing is not Flat racing with a few obstacles in the way. It is one of racing's favourite clichés that 'they are there to be jumped', and, like most clichés, it became one because it contains an unavoidable truth.

Winning hurdle races is about fluent hurdling. How often have you seen good horses off the Flat being beaten over hurdles by their supposed inferiors because one adapted to the new skill better than the other? An accomplished hurdler can take perhaps two lengths per flight off a clumsy one. Over the eight hurdles of a two-mile race 16 lengths is a lot to give away, whatever the relative merits on the Flat.

Potential hurdlers tend to come in two varieties: the horse directly off the Flat, and the purpose-bred jumping type which will need more time. Here it is important for the trainer to have the right horse for the right owner. Someone looking for immediate action will want the Flat horse ready to go. Someone else with more time, and perhaps more money, at his disposal will be prepared to invest patience in the specifically jumping-bred type.

However, both must be taught to observe the same principles. In the early stages, they will school over low poles, barely off the floor, to teach them the idea of leaving the ground and clearing an obstacle. As they learn the basics, so the obstacles become gradually more demanding until the horse has reached the necessary standard to appear on the racecourse.

Even then there remains the element of doubt. On its first appearance over hurdles, a horse must jump at racing pace, perhaps in a large field, two problems it will not have encountered before. Only after it has run can a trainer begin to judge its effectiveness as a hurdler. Horses can school perfectly at home only to be undone by the hurly-burly of the racecourse.

Hurdling can be taught, but only to a point. The truly natural, fast hurdler is born rather than made. Some faults can be ironed out, but without that indefinable agility a hurdler will not reach the top. The key, rather more than jumping, is speed away from the flight. All horses will get from one side of the hurdle to the other eventually, but the champions waste no time in regaining their racing stride again. Time spent in the air is wasted time.

Once a hurdler has grasped what is required of him, the trainer will school him only rarely. Unnecessary schooling can be a positive disadvantage as it increases the risk of injury. The horse will get all the practice he needs in racing, although the trainer may give him a quick refresher course over hurdles if he is having his first run for a while.

Steeplechasers need more schooling because their business demands greater accuracy for survival. Hurdlers often hit obstacles without coming to any harm, but for a chaser to mis-judge a fence badly is to threaten serious danger. Chasers must also be more versatile. They have to cope with plain fences, open ditches and water jumps. Failure to get to grips with them can mean a fall.

Inexperienced chasers, who have usually joined from the ranks of hurdlers, are best introduced at the less fashionable tracks where the fences tend to be easier to negotiate than at the top courses. The successful jumping of fences, more so than hurdles, is built on confidence. It will do a horse no good at all to suffer a crunching fall early in its career.

Falls, over both hurdles and fences, affect horses in different ways. Some pick themselves up as though nothing has happened; others take it very much to heart and need steady schooling before they are ready to venture on to the track again. Horses on the way back from a fall, or sometimes a series of falls, can be transparent. During a race it is easy to see them hesitating at fences, their confidence still not sufficiently restored for them to jump with any commitment.

Bringing a jumper back to fitness is usually more laborious than sharpening up a Flat racer. National Hunt horses are bigger and heavier than their Flat counterparts, and a summer out at grass can put on plenty of weight. That has to be worked off by steady roadwork, building firm muscle. They must then be cantered steadily, the pace increasing gradually to a peak of race-fitness. It is a lengthy process: a horse which returns to the stable at the end of July can take until October to be prepared for racing.

Stable visits

Visiting stables is guaranteed to quicken the pulse. Now the horse is in his working element, the trainer and his staff honing him into the finished article.

Stable life is hustle and bustle. Lads scurrying about their work, horses being pulled out of their boxes either for work or to be loaded into the horsebox to go racing, the trainer organising and giving instructions.

Although seeing your horse is a great day out, and one of the true pleasures of ownership, it is important to realise that you are in a working environment. Trainers should be pleased to see you, but certain courtesies need to be observed. Telephone first to let the trainer know you intend coming. If you just roll up un-announced you may catch him at a particularly bad time, or may not catch him at all. During the season, trainers often stay away if they have runners over several days at a distant meeting. When the sales are in full swing, trainers may again be absent from the yard for several days, or even out of the country.

Once you have set up the visit, you could ask when is a convenient time to watch the horse work. Trainers have distinct day-to-day patterns, so if you want to see your horse in full stride make sure you go down on a work morning. Watching work with trainers can be a sensitive subject. How a horse works is vital to a trainer's sense of its well-being: if a horse works sluggishly, it could be a sign that something is amiss.

Assessing work is a cornerstone of the trainer's art. Some trainers take themselves off to a quite corner to stand alone with their thoughts. Almost all are buried in concentration, trying to pick out any hint of a problem. A ceaseless stream of chatter from the visitor will not be welcomed.

In his excitement, it is easy for an owner to forget that his is not the only horse in the yard. The trainer has a responsibility to all his owners, and to live up to that he must be allowed to do his job properly.

That is not to say that owners should stand in the yard like cowed schoolboys in the headmaster's study. By all means play an active part in ownership. That is the whole point, but try to do it sensibly. Once you have got to know your trainer, you can come to an understanding which balances involvement with being a pest. Again, remember that his dealings with you will be multiplied perhaps 30 or 40 times, depending on how many owners he has in his stable. Trainers appreciate a little thought on this score. If you demonstrate an understanding of the way the stable works, he is far more likely to take notice of any observations you may have.

Some trainers will positively welcome an owner's views on his own horse. An owner has almost boundless time and enthusiasm for his own horse, whereas a trainer, no matter how much individual attention he devotes, cannot hope to copy an owner's scope for research in depth. If you have won the trainer's confidence, he should give some attention to your thoughts.

Although the trainer has the final responsibility for your horse, it is his lad who will deal with him more closely. Lads grow attached to the horses in their charge and should be encouraged. Always make a point of staying and chatting to the lad. Show him you are interested in what is going on, and that you value his efforts on your behalf. Giving him a present when you visit is good policy (the trainer will tell you how much and how often). Apart from showing your gratitude, it is human nature that if the lad has something at stake he is likely to take that little extra care.

There is a long-term value, to both lad and owner, in striking up a cheerful partnership. When new horses come into the stable it is not uncommon for lads to request to look after a particular owner's horse, or for an owner to ask for a lad with whom he gets on well.

Training fees

Having signed the training agreement (see Chapter 5) you will know the financial framework within which you and your trainer are to operate. The basic training fee is set in advance, but it is the additional charges which you will become much more aware of once the horse is actually in training.

Remember that a training fee is just that – a fee for a horse in training. The implication is not as obvious as it sounds. Although your horse may be in the yard, it may not necessarily be in serious training. If you have a particularly backward type which will take a considerable time to mature, or if your horse is recovering from an injury which will prevent it racing for the foreseeable future, there is no pressing need for it to be in the yard. Should you be in a situation in which your horse is likely to be off the racecourse for some time to come, ask your trainer about the possibility of sending it out of the yard to keep the fees down.

Many trainers can call upon small farms who will board the horse at lower rates until it is ready to come back into training proper. Some trainers will be keen to keep the horse in the yard whatever, simply to have the training fees coming in regularly. Unless there is a good reason for the horse staying with the trainer, it is unreasonable that the owner should have to keep paying out when he could be saving money.

The question is best illustrated during the respective close seasons. For Flat trainers, apart from those keeping horses busy through the all-weather racing programme, winter is a quiet time. Fillies are likely to be turned out, either returning to their owner's stud or being boarded elsewhere. However, the colts tend to stay in the stable. They can be much more of a handful, and if turned loose could injure themselves.

The National Hunt trainer's quiet period can range from April through to August, depending on how their horses react to the firm ground which becomes more prevalent during that period. Once the going becomes faster, horses who must have softer conditions need not be kept in full training.

This is one area in which National Hunt costs can be cheaper than the Flat. Jumpers, who, being older and often gelded, will tend to be more placid and can therefore be turned away during the long days of summer and need considerably less attention than Flat horses, either colts or fillies, require during the winter. Attention means money, so the jumper will cost less to oversee.

Veterinary charges are a great imponderable. A horse may go through its entire career without suffering any serious injury or illness. Unhappily it may be prone to mishap or be overtaken by an entirely unforeseen accident. Blacksmith charges can also vary from horse to horse. Like children, some are much heavier on shoes than others.

Travelling expenses will be another variable. Clearly, the more a horse runs, and the further away from home, the higher the travelling costs. When a horse is ready to run, it is not simply a case of putting it into a horsebox and waving goodbye. The trainer may have his own box, or he may have to use an independent transport company. In either case, he should be looking to send more than one horse to keep the costs down.

There is also the matter of travelling expenses for the lads. The lad who looks after the horse will, of course, go. He will probably be accompanied by a travelling head lad, whose function is to oversee the smooth running of the trip. The trainer could also go, although it depends on his commitments elsewhere. Many of the leading trainers rarely visit run-of-the-mill meetings.

If a trainer does attend, he is entitled to claim expenses. Thus, not only does the horse travel, so too does a team of lads and possibly the trainer. Costs can escalate rapidly. When a horse runs at a distant meeting, an overnight stay may be involved for the staff. Aside from the travelling allowances, the horse has to be shod with racing plates, so a blacksmith's fee is also incurred.

Trying to cut costs in this area is probably false economy. Having gone through, and paid for, all the previous stages, now that the horse has reached the racecourse it deserves to be given its best chance. If only one lad travels, there is little room for manoeuvre should something else happen which requires attention. That is not to say that bills should be paid blindly. There is room here for creative accounting on the part of any trainer who is less than scrupulous. One owner new to racing found himself with a bill for travelling on the basis of his being the only horse sent to the meeting. A closer look showed that the trainer had sent three horses to the meeting.

Receiving a bill for your horse being the trainer's only runner at a meeting is hardly a suggestion of malpractice, but if it happens regularly he should be tackled as to why he is not making more effort to travel in numbers. The trainer should also be looking into the possibility of sharing a horsebox with other trainers' runners sent from the same centre.

Some trainers have a habit of imposing deductions from prize-money in addition to those laid down in the Rules. This cannot be justified. The percentage payments are structured to reward all those involved, including owner, trainer, jockey and stable staff. Should the owner wish to give any of the team a present, that is entirely at his discretion. It is not the trainer's right to help himself – so be sure you are aware of his policy, and his reasons.

A trainer may also try to collect a commission on the sale price of a horse. Again, this should be discouraged as a general principle. If a trainer has, by his own skills and those of his staff, made your horse more valuable than when it was bought, it is not unreasonable for him to expect a small percentage of the difference between the buying and selling price. However, it is totally unacceptable for a trainer to demand a percentage of the sale price regardless of the arithmetic. If an owner has lost money on the horse, he cannot be expected to hand over a portion of whatever is left to the trainer. Remember, if the trainer has failed to bring the best out of the horse, he may not be totally blameless in its decline in value. That he should expect to be paid for it as well is preposterous.

The coup

Lord Hippo suffered fearful loss
By putting money on a horse
Which he believed, if it were pressed,
Would run far faster than the rest*

Belloc's cautionary tale should never be far from the thoughts of anyone attempting a coup. Although the gambling Lord Hippo saved the day in the end, life does not always offer such neat deliverance.

The desire to reach deep into bookmakers' satchels is an urge felt by most owners. But being on the inside as an owner is a long way short of a licence to do so. Although the Press loves to record tales of coups that are landed, it is, in the main, the successful ones that are reported. Many more fail and go largely unrecorded.

To land a gamble, there are two critical considerations: to have

*Reproduced by permission of the Peters, Fraser & Dunlop Group Ltd

the right horse and, perhaps more important, to have the right trainer. It is a waste of time dreaming about a betting coup if your horse can barely get out of its own way. No matter how generous a price an owner may secure, it only counts if the horse wins. The two elements, horse and trainer, are inseparable. The trainer will recognise in his yard a horse which, in the case of a handicap, is weighted below its true value. Once he is aware of that potential, a campaign can be planned, aimed at a victory generously supported by the owner's money.

One definition of a coup is 'a brilliant and successful stroke', which hardly applies if the win is so obvious everyone can see it coming. The very nature of a coup is that it should be kept discreet, so those involved can put their money on at the highest price available. If your prime aim is to pull off a betting coup, you must choose your trainer carefully. Some trainers are adept at preparing a horse to win a specific race; others, it must be said, would not know a well-handicapped horse if one bit them.

Anyone with even a passing knowledge of racing will quickly become aware of trainers who run what are generally described as gambling stables. That is not to say that every horse such a trainer runs has been especially trained to win the race in which it is competing. It is more widely applied to particular instances when a horse has as much as possible in its favour and is thought likely to win. A gambling stable can be expected to make the most of such an opportunity.

Early-season races on the Flat can be a profitable hunting ground. Horses can mature appreciably over the winter, developing the strength to realise their potential. Their form for the previous year may be left behind simply because they have grown up. National Hunt horses are less likely to show almost overnight improvement. They are usually older and will have already had a fair amount of racing, so the scope for instant progress is greatly reduced.

As secrecy is the foundation on which a successful coup is built, it is important to know how the trainer works in giving information to the owners in his stable. Some will tell only the owner of a particular horse if it is fancied. Others, mostly smaller trainers, will let all the owners in the stable in on what is happening. It is vital to be sure of how you stand. There is the story of a group of owners who were horrified to read that their trainer had landed a massive gamble with another owner, without sharing the information. The trainer acted quickly to notify all the owners in his yard that they were privy only to information concerning their own horses.

Some trainers are happy for owners to telephone and ask if a particular horse is fancied, regardless of who owns it. The trainer will tell them how he feels, but there is no guarantee of success. One owner availed himself of his trainer's opinions, only to find that 25 apparently fancied runners produced a grand total of two winners.

There is the other side of the coin, where a trainer tells an owner his horse has no chance, only for it to win. Far from savouring an unexpected triumph, the owner, particularly if he likes to bet on his horses, is more likely to be incandescent with rage. There is always the lingering doubt that the trainer knew all about it, but withheld the information to back it himself. In the overwhelming majority of cases that is just not true. Horses are unpredictable and will regularly confound those closest to them.

The unexpected lies in wait for even the most carefully planned coup. A horse can be baulked in running. In the case of jump races it can be brought down through no fault of its own. It may just find one better on the day.

There is no middle ground. The adroitly-executed gamble is celebrated loudly and gloriously with anyone who cares to listen. If it comes unstuck, even by the width of a cigarette paper, all the losers can do is turn and walk away quietly. Or perhaps not so quietly. One unfortunate owner in Buenos Aires staked his life savings on a touted good thing, only to see it trail in last. As the horse returned to the unsaddling enclosure, the thwarted backer leapt the rail, drew a gun and at point-blank range shot the hapless beast between the eyes.

5: Registrations

With the horse bought and placed with a trainer, it is now time to satisfy the Jockey Club's regulations on ownership. Your trainer should guide you, but there is no harm in understanding the essentials.

To be eligible to run a horse under the Rules of Racing, an owner must comply with five basic requirements:

to be a registered owner
to have registered his colours
to have registered the name of the horse he wishes to enter
if the horse is in the care of a licensed trainer, to have signed a
  training agreement with that trainer
to have registered an authority for the trainer to act on the
  owner's behalf

Registration as an owner should be addressed to the Jockey Club's Portman Square, London, headquarters, but the remaining four are dealt with by Weatherbys, based at Wellingborough (see Useful Addresses, page 133). Weatherbys are secretaries to the Jockey Club, acting in effect as racing's civil service, administering the sport under their contract with the Jockey Club. It is an association dating back to 1770, when James Weatherby was invited to become Keeper of the Match-Book, Stakeholder and Secretary to the Jockey Club.

The registrations are held by Weatherbys, but are granted and authorised by the Stewards of the Jockey Club. The fees from the registrations go to the Jockey Club for the administration of racing. Attempts to short-cut the system are virtually guaranteed to fail. Weatherbys operate an intricate series of cross-checks on entries and if the necessary requirements are not met, the entry will not be accepted.

Registering as an owner

By the often maze-like standards of officialdom, the application form is brief and comprehensible, although a certain depth of information is required. After the standard name, address and telephone number series of questions, details of other names by which you are known (stage names, noms de plume, for example) and additional residences are required.

Occupation and position must be given, although some married women may bridle at the instruction that, if they are not in business on their own account, their husband's occupation should be provided. The emancipated woman clearly cuts little ice at Portman Square. That same direction carries the somewhat quaint note that 'Gentleman' and 'Merchant' are not considered sufficiently descriptive. Where applicable, details of having been declared a bankrupt or a criminal conviction, other than a motoring offence, must be furnished. A criminal record is, in itself, not enough to have an application turned down, but the potential owner may be asked to attend an interview with the licensing stewards.

Should you be re-applying for registration, details of previous racehorse owning experience will be required, including if you have run horses under a different name, such as a maiden name, a different surname by marriage or deed-poll. Also required are the names and addresses of two referees, preferably connected with racing or holding professional qualifications.

Application for registration as an owner carries a once-only charge of £29.00 plus VAT. However, the registration will lapse after a period of 24 consecutive months without a horse in training, and the process must then be repeated for re-registration.

Registrations

Registering colours

To have one's colours carried is synonymous with racehorse ownership. They are, in effect, the family crest and will be the strongest visual contact between horse and owner while the race is being run. Remember that colours are primarily for identification, a theme which runs throughout the Jockey Club's policy towards colours and governs what is acceptable.

To register a set of colours with the Jockey Club costs £15.00 plus VAT. Once the colours have been accepted they are registered annually on 1 January, and can be kept regardless of whether an owner still has a horse in training as long as they are re-registered. It is not uncommon for famous racing dynasties, who may not have runners at a particular time but expect relatives to return to the sport in the future, to continue registering colours. This keeps the livery in the family name and prevents it becoming public property, and probably irretrievable, in the meantime.

Colours are due for registration on 1 January each year, not one year after they were first registered. If, for example, they are accepted in November and used even just once you will be liable for the full fee again in the New Year. If the colours are registered late in the year and not used, the Jockey Club can use its discretion and waive the subsequent year's fee. It has no obligation to do so, however, and the prospective owner is advised to keep an eye on his horse's training timetable. If there is little chance of any entries being made before the New Year, it is safer to wait until then before registering colours.

Once the decision to go ahead has been taken, there are four basic elements, each regulated by the Jockey Club, to be considered: the colours to be used, and the designs which may be incorporated into the body (jacket), sleeves and cap. The colours themselves must be selected from a set of 18, arranged on the registration form rather like a decorator's chart. The jacket design must conform to one of 27 laid down. So too must the sleeves (from 12 agreed designs) and the cap (from a group of 10).

Mind-boggling cocktails of form and style will founder on the official view that clarity is king. The attempted use of any motif which is not immediately identifiable by the racecourse officials,

including the commentator, is doomed to failure. However close to an owner's heart a horse may be, racing's existence is based on knowing at first glance which horse is which.

Although the options nowadays are strictly governed, exceptions remain which pre-date the international agreements on colours first enforced some 20 years ago. Mrs Miles Valentine's marvellous cherry hearts on a pink background would no longer be allowable, nor would Pat Muldoon's McIntyre tartan and red sleeves carried to successive Champion Hurdle victories by Sea Pigeon. The Stewards will, however, sanction colours registered with a recognised overseas turf authority, even if they do not conform to the patterns laid down in this country, for foreign-trained horses contesting races here.

Currently there are some 14,000 sets of colours. Those unwittingly identical or similar to existing colours will be turned down. The Jockey Club does not consider a cap to be a distinguishing feature, except when an owner is running two horses in the same race.

The simplest way to save time and effort in ensuring that your choice of colours is available is to telephone Weatherbys, who keep a complete record of colours already in existence on computer. You will be informed, literally within minutes, of those combinations still available, and of what alterations to your original choice may be required to make them acceptable. Once you have verbal confirmation of your colours, you can fill in the official Jockey Club registration form, on which you must give both a written description of the colours and design and mark them on a silhouette of a rider's body.

However, you have not registered your colours until written acceptance has been received. It is best to wait until then before having colours made. A last-minute hitch could leave you with a set which is worthless. A set of colours, incorporating jacket and cap, will range from upwards of around £60 depending on the difficulty of the design. There are specialist companies but a number of saddlers also produce colours. Although the term 'silks' is applied to racing colours generally, they are available in several materials. Silks are the most expensive and are best suited to the warmer, drier summer conditions of Flat racing. A weather-proof material is probably a better year-round bet as the colours can be more comfortably worn under both codes.

Over the last 18 months there has been a growth in interest in aerodynamic colours, which stretch to fit the jockey's shape and thus, in theory at least, reduce wind resistance. Their case remains unproven, although they have a powerful advocate in the brilliant American trainer, D. Wayne Lukas. There is nothing to stop you experimenting with them. They may look inelegant, but will not do the horse's chance any harm. In terms of price they sit between the weatherproofs and silks.

Woollen colours, most commonly used in National Hunt racing, are in decline. They can shrink after a soaking and are less easy to remove in the event of an injury to a jockey than the newer styles.

To produce a set of colours, regardless of make and style, will take about two weeks, although some companies offer an express 48 hour service, usually at extra cost.

Registration of names

Here is endless scope for humour, sharp observation, self-promotion or any other heart's desire. The Queen is among the wittiest in naming her horses. In recent years she has offered us, among others, Hall Of Mirrors (by Clever Trick out of Reflection) and Maroon (by Roan Rocket out of Mulberry Harbour).

Louis Freedman, the owner of the Derby winner Reference Point, is another to exercise his mind fruitfully in this direction. Lowawatha (by Dancing Brave out of Shorthouse) is among the latest additions to a droll list. Freedman also had great fun with his mare Seventh Bride, whose offspring included One Over Parr and Polygamy.

Naming trends are not uncommon among the bigger owners. Lady Beaverbrook is fond of giving her runners seven-letter names – Boldboy, Bustino and Riboson being among those to represent her illustriously. The Aga Khan pursues a policy of beginning a name with the first letter of the dam's name, which produced his Derby winners Shergar, Shahrastani and Kahyasi, out of the mares Sharmeen, Shademah and Kadissya respectively.

Whichever method you embrace, it must be done within certain

JACKET

1 Plain	2 Seams	3 Epaulets	4 Stripe	5 Braces	6 Stripes	7 Hoop
			4" centre strip	2" vertical strip	Alternate 2" vertical stripes	4" hoop

8 Hoops	9 Halved	10 Quartered	11 Sash	12 Cross Belts	13 Chevron	14 Chevrons
Alternated 2" hoops	Vertically only sleeves reversed		4" diagonal stripe from left shoulder to right hip	4" diagonal stripe from each shoulder	One large "V"	Alternate 2" chevrons

15 Check	16 Diamonds	17 Spots	18 Stars	19 Cross of Lorraine	20 Diamond	21 Star
1"-1½" squares	4" vertical diamonds	Spots 2½" in diameter	Stars 3" in diameter	10" solid cross	10" vertical diamond	10" solid star

22 Disc	23 Inverted Triangle	24 Diabolo	25 Large Spots	26 Triple Diamond	27 Hollow Box	
10" solid disc	10" triangle	Triangles of same size	4" spots from right shoulder to left hip	6" vertical diamond	10" box	

SLEEVES

1 Plain	2 Armlet	3 Hooped	4 Striped
5 Chevrons	6 Seams	7 Stars	8 Spots
9 Halved	10 Diabolo	11 Diamonds	12 Check

4" Vertical diamonds   1-1½" squares

CAP

1 Plain	2 Hooped	3 Striped
4 Check	5 Spots	6 Quartered
7 Star	8 Diamond	9 Stars
4" centre to apex	4" centre to apex	
10 Diamonds		

Designs which may be incorporated into owners' colours
(reproduced by courtesy of Weatherbys)

strictly defined limits, propriety not the least of them. A maximum of 18 characters, including spaces, may be used, which accounts for such eyesores as Whenyourtrainsgone and more recently Lastofthebrownies and Weareagrandmother. Names may not be repeated, for the obvious reason of confusion, so any name which is already registered will be refused. Nor will similar-sounding names be admitted. A name cannot be defamatory, ambiguous or rude, although owners rarely tire of trying to slip one through the net in the last category. The names of famous people may be used only with their written permission, and similarly horses may only be named after a trade product with that company's permission.

As with colours, Weatherbys can also confirm by telephone whether a name will be acceptable. They will first ascertain if the name is available, and then check that it is not too close to an existing name. Although your choice may be unique, it may sound similar to another name when spoken.

Be prepared to exercise patience as well as imagination. There are around 250,000 names currently registered, some of them permanently protected and others released only after a lengthy delay. The names of Classic winners are protected, so forget lining up Mill Reef or Brigadier Gerard. Even then the waiting list for making names available is formidable. The names of stallions and broodmares are protected for 25 and 15 years respectively after death or after being retired from stud duties. Other horses for 10 years after death.

If no death is reported, a stallion's name is protected until his 45th birthday, a broodmare until her 35th, and the 25th for the remainder. The process is one of trial and error. One regularly thwarted owner, after racking his brains for inspiration, could eventually respond to another rejection with only a resigned: 'Well that's the end of number 31'. He did eventually succeed.

The form for the registration of a horse's name includes provision for its markings to be detailed by a veterinary surgeon. If you have placed the horse with a trainer, he will arrange for that part of the form to be completed. All you need worry about is providing up to four names, in order of preference, assuming you have not previously liaised with Weatherbys.

Registrations

Names cannot be registered before the horse is a yearling – that is, one year old on 1 January. However, if you have come up with a particularly appropriate name and fear it may be taken, a name can be reserved for a fee of £16.50 plus VAT. The scale of registration charges, all plus VAT, varies in accordance with the horse's age: £16.50 under two years old, £33.00 two and three years old, £27.50 four years old and upwards, and £140.00 to change a name (although this may be done only if a horse has not already raced under a registered name and has not appeared as a named horse in the General Stud Book, the register of Thoroughbred births).

It may well be a myth that horses with ugly names never win big races (how can a horse know what its name is?) but the fact that there are relatively few around with truly embarrassing names suggests that owners see their horses as things of beauty, and are prepared to invest some time and thought into bestowing names worthy of the ideal.

The training agreement

An owner, or in the case of a partnership each owner, must enter into a training agreement on the fees to be charged. The agreement must then be registered with the Jockey Club. The basic agreement is precisely that – a basic agreement and no more. The owner and trainer agree a rate per week per horse, with, where applicable, the fee to be divided among the partners commensurate with their respective shares.

Other than the basic costs, the agreement also embraces a host of extras which are almost impossible to define precisely in advance. On the reverse of the form is a list outlining further areas of expenditure: horse transport by transporter's account or by mileage if the trainer's own box is used, trainer's expenses, blacksmith, veterinary treatment, gallop fees (if not included in the basic agreement), and so on. They are simply marked to signify that the trainer will incorporate those costs in the total bill.

Under the agreement, the owner acknowledges that the trainer may vary his fees but in that eventuality the trainer must notify in writing both the owner and Weatherbys. The owner has three weeks in which to accept or reject the new agreement. If he chooses to reject it, the original agreement will be deemed to be at an end and the horse or horses concerned will not be allowed to run until a new agreement is registered.

The trainer will register the agreement, at £4.50 plus VAT, the only one of the five basic requirements for which he is directly responsible for payment.

Although a bare presentation of the facts suggests that trainers can hold an owner to ransom, in practice that is not the case. Trainers, by and large, are not naive enough to think that they can consistently raise fees without a murmur from the owner. If it does happen and you are dissatisfied with an increase in the rate, you still have the ultimate sanction of taking the horse somewhere else. Apart from the mountainous paperwork involved in having to register a stable's-worth of new agreements, trainers try to avoid upsetting owners deeply enough to encourage them to leave.

Authority to act

An authority to act allows a trainer to act on an owner's behalf. Mostly it will concern making entries.

Owners can enter their own horses but it is a time-consuming business, and the vast majority prefer to leave it in the hands of the trainer. In a partnership, only one of the partners need sign the authority. Registration of an authority to act is £19.50 plus VAT.

The racing account

For the new owner, these registrations are likely to be the first administrative costs incurred. To facilitate these payments, and others such as entry fees, an owner will require the accounting services offered by either Weatherbys, the Jockey Club or Pratt and Co, which is based at Haywards Heath, Sussex.

About 70 per cent of the racing accounts are held by Weatherbys, 29 per cent by the Jockey Club and the remaining 1 per cent by Pratt and Co. Weatherbys do, in fact, administer all three, and distribute the figures where required to the other two, because all the registrations, entries and so on are handled by them.

Registrations

Although a Weatherbys account is often mentioned in the same breath as ownership, an owner does not have to have his account with Weatherbys. He may use whichever he likes, but there are differences between Weatherbys and the Jockey Club. Pratt and Co offers a similar service to Weatherbys.

With a Jockey Club account, statements are produced either fortnightly or monthly. On the statement, only items under the Rules of Racing may be entered, that is, registration, entry and jockey fees. No payments to third parties can be included, such as payments to trainers. No money is required in advance.

The period of credit is short, and the account is payable virtually by return of post. If the account is unpaid after a statement and a reminder, the Jockey Club has the power to 'stop a horse at scale' meaning that the next time the horse runs the owner will be told to pay the outstanding balance to the Clerk of the Scales on the day it runs. In most cases, the owner will pay, but if not he will be penalised.

Should the owner continue to run up fees without paying, he will be put on the Forfeit List, which is published in the *Racing Calendar*. Once an owner appears on the list, he becomes a disqualified person, no longer able to take part in racing. Entries will no longer be accepted, registrations will lapse and the owner, by now a former owner, is not allowed on the racecourse.

On the brighter side, credit balances are paid twice a month, although prize-money is not due until 15 days after the race meeting to allow time for dope tests, objections or anything else which may affect the result.

To open a Weatherbys account, £200 is required in advance. From that, Weatherbys will pay anyone the owner instructs them to, meeting, for example, training fees, vets' bills, transport charges. Payments which have nothing to do with racing will also be administered, provided Weatherbys are given the authority. If a Weatherbys account becomes overdrawn, an owner's liabilities will be met for longer than under the Jockey Club system. However, as with any commercial company, that situation will not be allowed to continue indefinitely. If an owner does default on a Weatherbys account, Weatherbys will sue through the courts in common with the pursuit of any debt. Because of the greater latitude on credit, statements are produced either monthly, or quarterly.

Again reflecting its commercial status, Weatherbys charge administration fees whereas there is no charge for a Jockey Club account. Under the Weatherbys system, bank base rate is levied on overdrawn accounts, and for every line of narration on the statement, such as entries, there is a line charge of around 45p, which rises broadly in line with inflation. However, if the account remains in credit of £250 or more, a notional interest will be off-set against charges incurred. Administration charges, comprising a combination of lines of narration and any overdrawn interest, are added to the account half-yearly.

When an owner's first expense, usually a registration, has been incurred, Weatherbys confirm the expenditure and offer the opportunity to open an account with them. If an owner fails to state a preference for any of the three available methods, then he will, by default, be put on the Jockey Club system.

6: Types of races

There is a saying that there is a race for every horse. That is not strictly true. There will never be a shortage of unfortunates who would not win if they started yesterday. But a horse's winning prospects can be maximised by careful study of the races available, and by running in those races in which it has the best chance. To borrow another popular racing chestnut: keep yourself in the best company and your horse in the worst.

Entering a horse in suitable races is not as obvious as it sounds. Every season, Flat and National Hunt, horses are regularly asked to contest races they have no possible chance of winning. The reasons vary: some owners want to have runners at the top tracks, some prefer not to travel to find the best opportunity, often trainers over-estimate the ability of their horses.

Owners' motivation is a recurring theme, and here is another aspect. How much do you want to win a race? Will you send a horse trained in Newmarket to Carlisle, bearing in mind the transport costs, if a suitable opening occurs there? Do you run the horse even if you cannot watch it? Do you mind running the horse in bad races on minor courses? Those questions must be addressed most seriously by owners of moderate horses. For the owner of a moderate horse, picking and choosing races is but a pipe-dream. In the placing of horses is one of the sharpest skills of training. Once the horse's merit is established, it is up to the trainer to unearth the more realistic opportunities for success.

There was a neat illustration of this early in the 1990 Flat season. Jimmy Etherington, a trainer based in Malton, was struggling to find the right race for Superbrave, a four-year-old sprinter which had never won. Eventually he did – 300 miles away at Folkestone. However, with the target identified, Etherington wasted no time in despatching Superbrave south. Superbrave did his bit by winning. Such initiative will not always have a happy ending, but it demonstrates the possibilities. Races can be won from unpromising positions, granted solid research by the trainer and co-operation from the owner.

The story also underlines another truth of placing horses: Etherington went to Folkestone because it was markedly the best opportunity he could find for Superbrave. There would have been no point in undertaking the trip if the horse had had only the same chance as he would have had virtually next door to the stable at, say, Thirsk or Ripon. Casting the net wide is an important option for owner and trainer, but should be used only when circumstances are in their favour.

Another aspect of placement is when horses begin their career. This applies to horses of greater and lesser talents. Some trainers are noted, notorious perhaps, for starting horses off in red-hot races on the top tracks. It can prove counter-productive. If the trainer has over-rated the horse, there is little chance of success. If the horse is well beaten, it will tell him little about his ability. Should the trainer continue to campaign in good races, there is also the danger the horse can become soured by constantly being asked to do too much.

A wiser policy is to start at the bottom and work up. Even the top trainers have favourite smaller tracks on which to introduce their potential superstars. Henry Cecil used Nottingham for subsequent fillies' Triple Crown winner Oh So Sharp's first race. The outstanding miler of 1989, Zilzal, trained by Michael Stoute, made his debut at Leicester. Guy Harwood often uses Salisbury to blood his leading two-year-olds. The best horses do not have to start in the best company.

That strategy is not confined to aspiring champions. At any

level, an early success gives a horse the confidence on which his career can be built. Starting at the bottom and working up is a better method of development than beginning at the top and working down.

However, a horse's characteristics, some more distinctive than others, may have to be discovered by trial and error. Some prefer to race in a particular direction: Desert Orchid, who is much happier turning right-handed, is a notable example. Others have marked going preferences, being better on either fast or soft ground. Almost all will have a best distance which may take time to pin-point. Even the best may be subject to this last problem. Ajdal, the 1987 champion sprinter, ran unsuccessfully in the Derby before Michael Stoute brought him back to the shorter distances which suited him so admirably.

The Classics of the Flat racing season – the 1,000 Guineas, 2,000 Guineas, Derby, Oaks and St Leger – are considered the supreme tests of the Thoroughbred. Restricted to three-year-olds, they range from the straight mile of the Guineas races at Newmarket, to the Epsom mile-and-a-half of the Derby and Oaks, concluding with the 1 mile 6 furlongs 127 yards of the St Leger at Doncaster.

All five are open to fillies, with the 1,000 Guineas and Oaks for fillies only. The greatest Classic achievement for a colt is to complete the Triple Crown by winning the three races open to him – the 2,000 Guineas, the Derby and the St Leger. Nijinsky was the last to do so in 1970, although the decline in importance of the St Leger suggests that modern owners hold the Triple Crown less dearly. In 1989, Nashwan, having taken the 2,000 Guineas and the Derby, was prepared instead for the Prix de l'Arc de Triomphe, a more highly-regarded race internationally, at Longchamp. In the event, defeat in a preparatory race meant he missed that engagement too.

There is also the fillies' Triple Crown comprising the 1,000 Guineas, Oaks and St Leger, last completed by Oh So Sharp in 1985. Twice fillies have won four Classics: Formosa (1868) and Sceptre (1902) both took the 1,000 Guineas, 2,000 Guineas, Oaks and St Leger. Nowadays, however, trainers tend to keep their fillies to the 1,000 Guineas and Oaks, although the St Leger regularly attracts high-class fillies.

Pattern races form the framework which caters for the best horses. On the Flat, the races are collected together as groups, from Group One to Group Three. The Group One races are the championship events. They include the Classics and those races designed to test merit at the highest level. Group Two races are just below championship standard but are still important in an international context. At Group Three, the standard is slightly lower than the other two categories, and this type of race tends to have greater significance in the domestic programme rather than internationally. Below this third tier lies the programme of 'Listed Races', in effect a fourth level of the Pattern.

Pattern races cut across all boundaries of age, sex and distance. There are Pattern races for two-year-olds, three-year-olds and older horses, and for sprinters, middle-distance horses and stayers. Some are limited to fillies, and some to specific age groups, most notably the Classics. However, as the season progresses, the Pattern provides the stage on which the various generations may be judged. The Eclipse Stakes at Sandown and the King George VI & Queen Elizabeth Diamond Stakes at Ascot are two prestigious mid-term events which pit the top-class three-year-olds against their elders. By watching the various age groups in competition, the comparative quality of their generations can be evaluated.

The Flat Pattern is constructed at an international level, embracing the racing authorities of Great Britain, Ireland, France, Germany and Italy. Each country stages its own Group races but they are open to overseas competition.

National Hunt racing also has a Pattern system, but it differs fundamentally in several ways. Jump racing is almost entirely domestic and therefore the Pattern applies only to Britain. British horses do run in Ireland, and vice versa, and there is some competition between Britain and France, but it is tiny compared to the regular international raids launched during the Flat season. Also, there is no pressing need to compare various generations of National Hunt horses. Their careers are much longer than their

Flat counterparts, so the question of age rarely enters the argument. And as the vast majority are geldings, there are no breeders to satisfy with immediate assessments of excellence.

The jumping Pattern, which has been reconstructed for the 1990–91 season, is built around two peaks: Christmas, when Kempton puts on the King George VI Chase and the Christmas Hurdle, and Wetherby holds the Castleford Chase; and March and April when, first Cheltenham and then Liverpool each holds festivals of high-class racing. The top races are divided into Grades One, Two and Three: Grade One are championship races, Grade Two are slightly less important but Grade Three are high-grade handicaps such as the Hennessy Gold Cup, Whitbread Gold Cup and Grand National which have considerable significance. There are no handicaps in the Flat Pattern.

A *Sporting Life* book, 'A Guide to the Pattern', gives a full explanation of the Flat racing Pattern.

Handicaps, either Flat or National Hunt, are designed to give all horses an equal chance by allotting them differing weights. The better a horse, the more weight he has to carry.

Horses are given handicap ratings which reflect their ability. To qualify for a rating, a horse must have run a minimum of three times or won a race. A horse which does not meet those qualifications is allowed to run in a handicap under National Hunt rules, but will automatically be allotted top weight. A horse cannot carry automatic top weight in Flat racing.

Handicaps are framed by reference to the ratings of horses eligible to run in them. For example, a handicap described as 'for horses rated 0–80' means that any horse with a rating on or between those limits can enter. The greater the horse's ability, the higher handicap rating he will be given. So the higher the top limit in the race conditions, the better the class of horse which may be entered. Each horse is re-assessed regularly on its performances. If it shows improved form, it will be given a higher rating and said to be 'going up the weights'. If, on the other hand, a horse continues to run below its previous form, it will be given a lower rating and go 'down the weights'.

There is a constant duel between trainers and handicappers.

Trainers regularly accuse the handicappers of giving a horse too much weight and therefore making it extremely difficult for that horse to win a handicap. The handicappers, who are always ready to look at individual cases if there is a grievance, reply that each horse is treated strictly on its merits.

Perhaps the biggest bone of contention is when trainers argue that handicappers are quick to raise a horse but a good deal slower to bring it down again. The mechanics of the system make that almost inevitable. If a horse runs above its previous form, the handicapper will almost certainly increase its rating on the basis that it is improving. If he chose to ignore it, imagine the furore from other owners claiming that a particular horse had been preferentially treated. The problem is centred on the fact that, while one good run can be sufficient grounds for a handicapper to raise a horse, one bad run is not necessarily grounds for immediately lowering the rating. Handicappers often defer judgement, particularly if that horse has shown good form in the past.

Getting a horse well handicapped, that is, on a rating which is below its true merit, is a fine art – preferably without resorting to blatant cheating, although it would be ingenuous to imagine that does not happen on occasion. How may a trainer try to persuade the handicapper his horse is not as good as it really is? A horse may be run over a distance short of, or further than, its best; on a course which it does not like; or on ground on which it is uncomfortable. When the desired rating has been achieved, the horse will find itself running over its best trip on its preferred ground, and showing apparently miraculous improvement!

A more subtle method is to win small races with a good horse, although this has become more difficult to pull off. Handicappers long underestimated form at the less fashionable tracks, especially on the Flat, and so allocated winners a rating below their real ability. Luca Cumani noticed this and quickly became a master at exploiting the loophole. Talented horses were dispatched north to win modest races, not for the prize-money but to secure a favourable handicap mark for more valuable events later on. They were then able to put together a string of successes before the handicapper finally got to grips with them.

Cumani, an excellent trainer by any standards, has found it

almost impossible to get away with the same ploy nowadays. Handicappers have got wiser and are constantly on the look-out for the tactic, whoever may try to use it.

Maiden races are for horses, regardless of age or sex, which have not won a race. They are run under both Flat and National Hunt rules, but a horse can run in some maiden races under one code even if it has won under the other. Maiden races under National Hunt rules, for example, are frequently contested by horses which have won on the Flat.

The standing of maiden races differs between Flat and jumps. Over jumps, the maiden hurdles and chases cater for the very moderate class of horse which has been unable to make its mark in better company. On the Flat, maiden races serve as the launch-pad for most horses, particularly two-year-olds. It is standard practice to introduce two-year-olds and, indeed, three-year-olds if they have been too backward to race as juveniles, at this level. Although maiden races vary in quality from course to course (a Newmarket maiden will be much harder to win than one at Edinburgh), they offer a largely predictable standard of competition. There will be no previous winners in the race. Those which have already run can be judged by a glance at their form and there will be some newcomers, although they will decrease in the second-half of the season as more horses start to race. Once a horse has run in a maiden, a trainer should have a yardstick by which he can plan the next step of a horse's career.

A former extension of maiden races, the maiden at closing, in which horses who had not won when the race closed were eligible, has been overtaken by graduation races. They were introduced as a stepping stone for horses to progress from winning maiden races to tackling stronger opposition.

Selling and Claiming races are the lowest rung on the ladder of competition. Claiming races sit just above selling races. The mechanics of the two categories are discussed in Chapter 3, from the standpoint of an owner considering buying a horse out of either race.

An owner wishing to retain the winner of a selling race could be in for a shock. The owner keeps the prize-money, but not all of the selling price. In all selling races, horses are entered to be sold for a set figure equal to the added prize-money of the race. However, if the horse wins convincingly and is sold for a sum in excess of that figure, the surplus is divided equally between the owner and the racecourse.

Claiming races are governed by a more complex calculation. Each horse is entered to be claimed for not less than a certain figure, which is calculated according to the race conditions (remember the horse does not have to win to be claimed). The owner keeps the claiming price of his horse, less 10 per cent which goes to the racecourse. He also receives 15 per cent of the surplus, plus any prize-money he may have won.

An owner may claim his own horse back, and if he chooses to do so the calculation works in reverse. As he will be receiving the claiming price himself, he pays 10 per cent of that price, plus 85 per cent of any surplus.

It is easy to see the importance of sellers and claimers to race-course finances. Until quite recently many of the smaller courses survived only on the profits they received from sellers, and even now they remain opposed to any suggestions that such races be phased out.

Apprentice/Amateur Riders' races are limited to the appropriate category of rider. Fledgling jockeys are known as apprentices on the Flat and conditional riders over jumps. They have their own races designed to give them more experience without having to take on the top-flight jockeys.

Even within that category, apprentice and conditional races can vary. The race conditions may state, for example, that it is confined to apprentices who have not ridden more than 10 winners, which disqualifies the more experienced apprentices. Apprentices receive a weight allowance when riding against professionals, but there are also allowances within apprentice races themselves. In our example, an apprentice who has not ridden a winner at all may be allowed to claim 5lb to give him a better chance.

Amateur riders' races are run under both Flat and National

Hunt rules. They are more popular over jumps because amateurs are allowed to ride against professionals in other races and so have the opportunity to gain more experience. Also, National Hunt owners sometimes keep a horse with a view to riding it in races themselves. On the Flat, amateurs can compete *only* in amateur races. However, under both rules the weight range in amateurs' races differs from professional races. The bottom weight is usually higher to save amateurs from the starvation diets endured by many professional counterparts.

Guaranteed sweepstakes apply to the lower value races. The racecourse guarantees a set level of prize-money, regardless of the number of entries, but the entry fee for the owner is higher. Although, the racecourses may appear to be at risk, the category of race to which it applies usually attracts sufficient entries to prevent the course having to make up too great a difference between prize-money and entry fees.

Conditions races are non-handicaps governed by specific conditions. The weights may be framed according to the type of races or prize-money won. They often attract one or two good horses which are well-suited by the terms of the race, but can be uncompetitive if those horses frighten away the opposition.

The John Bull and the Jim Ford Chases at Wincanton are conditions races which regularly attract small though select fields.

Nursery handicaps are handicaps for two-year-olds which are run from July onwards. The maximum weight is 9st 7lb, exclusive of penalties.

Auction races are non-handicaps on the Flat in which the weights are decided by the purchase price at auction. The race conditions specify a top limit and any other restrictions to entry (for example, stating that the race is 'for horses sold as yearlings by public auction at sales in Great Britain or Ireland for not more than 10,000 guineas. For each 1,000 guineas paid below 10,000, there is an allowance of 1lb, to a maximum of 7lb').

The more cheaply the horse was bought, the less weight it

carries. The principle of auction races is to give owners of cheap yearlings an outlet to run their horses on favourable terms. With even the top price pitched relatively low, the big spenders are excluded.

A recent variation on the same theme is to use the selling price of a stallion's stock, rather than an individual sale, as the basis for the weights. Thus a horse by a less fashionable stallion will have less to carry than one whose stock has sold more expensively. All horses are eligible, regardless of whether they were bought at auction or not.

Novice hurdles and chases are restricted to horses which have not won either a hurdle or a chase respectively at the start of that season. Novice hurdles almost invariably attract big fields as they are the natural starting point for jumpers.

Unlike the concept of maidens, who cease to qualify for that description as soon as they have won a race, novices remain as such for the whole season. Novice hurdlers and chasers are eligible to run in that category as much as they want, although in practice multiple winners are discouraged from doing so by having to carry penalties. Penalties are generally imposed on the basis of races won. A successful novice hurdler may have to carry, say, an extra 7lb for each hurdle race won. Trainers are often prepared to run under a 7lb penalty, but once the horse has to start giving away a stone or more other opportunities will make greater appeal.

The same principles apply to novice chasers, who have mostly had some experience of hurdles previously. Once a horse starts novice chasing, the slate is wiped clean. Wins over hurdles are not carried forward to be included as penalties in novice chases.

National Hunt flat races, generally referred to as 'bumpers', are, paradoxically, flat races run under National Hunt rules. They are restricted to horses which have not run in any other type of race. Any horse which has run on the Flat, over hurdles or fences is automatically excluded. The idea is to provide opportunities for National Hunt-bred horses without their having to take on faster horses off the Flat, or more experienced jumpers. They act as a classroom where the first lessons can be learned, but horses may only run in a maximum of three of these races.

Well-intentioned though the idea may be, it has a serious flaw in restricting jockey arrangements to either conditional or amateur riders. If a young horse is to be educated, it should be given professional help, not be teamed with someone whose experience may be only marginally greater than its own. For all that, some very talented horses have come through the ranks. Forest Sun, the winner of the 1990 Waterford Crystal Supreme Novices Hurdle at Cheltenham, began his career in bumpers, as did Brown Chamberlin, the winner of the 1983 Hennessy Gold Cup at Newbury.

Weight-for-age

Weight-for-age is a scale of allowances by which horses receive weight from their elders. Older horses have matured and at level weights would have a major advantage over their juniors. To even out the generations, and allow them to compete against each other, the younger horses receive a weight concession. The allowance changes according to distance and time of year.

7: Entries

The entry of horses in the majority of races is based on the five-day system, which was introduced in November 1988. It applies to both Flat and National Hunt racing.

Entries, which are lodged with Weatherbys, must be finalised five days before the race is due to be run. That deadline is final. No amount of pleading or cajoling will persuade Weatherbys to re-open the race. There have been instances of trainers, or more accurately their secretaries, who usually deal with entries, leaving horses out of Classic races in error, and of fax messages apparently sent but not received. If an entry for a horse has not arrived by the appropriate time, no matter how great or small the race, it is simply tough luck.

Each racing day has its equivalent five-day stage, as illustrated below:

Schedule for entries

Race day	Race closes	Weights
Monday	Wednesday	Thursday
Tuesday	Thursday	Friday
Wednesday	Friday	Saturday
Thursday	Saturday	Sunday
Friday	Saturday	Sunday
Saturday	Monday	Tuesday

For example, if a race is scheduled for a Saturday, then the entries have to be in by noon on the preceding Monday. The basic schedule may change during unusually busy periods, such as Bank Holidays, but the above framework mostly holds good.

Once the entries, usually referred to simply as 'the five days', are completed, Weatherbys add the horses' weights for their respective races. The finished product is the basis of race fields.

The first stage, just the list of entries, is published in *The Sporting Life* on the day after the entry stage. Thus Saturday's entries are available, usually in alphabetical order, in Tuesday's newspaper. The more detailed fields, complete with weights and therefore in racecard order, are ready a day later. So, in the case of Saturday's racing, the information would be collated by Weatherbys on Tuesday and published in Wednesday's *Life*.

Although your trainer will probably be handling your horse's entries, it is worth knowing the cycle so that you can keep in touch with when and where your horse may run. It also gives you and your trainer the opportunity to size up the opposition and decide on the race which will best suit your horse.

Most entries are made over the telephone, although it is possible to enter by telex, fax transmission or letter. Anybody entering a horse must quote his security code – without it, the entry will not be accepted. Trainers and permit holders are issued with a coding as a matter of course, but if an owner fancies having a go at entering his own horses he must first apply for a security code. If the go-it-alone method appeals, make the entries by telephone. It is far easier to overcome any difficulties with someone at the other end of the line to advise you.

The five-day system involves only one payment, that being made upon entry. If the horse is withdrawn, the entry fee is forfeited. Races generally operate on an entry fee of one per cent of the 'added money', thus a £3,000 added race will cost £30 to enter. How the added money figure is arrived at is discussed in Chapter 8, which relates to prize-money.

Our example of £30 is not the end of the story. Additionally, there is a charge of £7.09 (plus VAT) which goes to the Jockey Club, and £1.20, forwarded to the Animal Health Trust in Newmarket. In certain races, mostly those at the bottom of the scale, there may also be surcharges on entry. The figures vary from race to race, but the charge increases in accordance with how many times the horse has run unplaced. The more unplaced runs, the higher the surcharge. Those races which carry a surcharge are noted in the *Racing Calendar.*

Money from surcharges goes into the Divided Race Fund, which finances the extra divisions when races are split in the interests of safety. Again, this applies primarily to lower grade contests.

When your horse has been safely entered at the five-day stage, it will have to be decided if he runs in the race in question. If the answer is yes, then he must be declared as a runner the day before at what is known as the overnight stage. The overnight stage is, in fact, a good deal earlier in the day: confirmation of running must be received by 10am in the summer, or 10.30am in winter.

At the overnight stage, the field for a race will be completed. The declared runners will be allotted their racecard numbers, sequentially from one to however many runners are in the field. Penalties, the extra weight given to horses which have won after the entry stage, will be added. The conditions of individual races specify how much more a horse must carry, usually based on the value of the race or races won. Blinkers, a visor, eyeshield or eyecover (mostly aids to a horse's concentration) must also be declared overnight.

Races which have attracted acceptors in excess of the safety figure will be divided where applicable. In races which are not divided, the field is reduced by balloting. This is usually done on the basis of the numbers of unplaced runs. The more of these your horse has, the greater the danger of being excluded should a ballot be necessary. If your horse is balloted out, the entry fee will be refunded. That, however, does not make up for the disappointment of missing a run. It is a sore point among owners that, when their horse is ready for action, it is frustrated by lack of opportunity.

Also, in handicaps, the weights are raised when necessary. If the top-weight at the five-day stage does not run, the highest-weighted horse remaining is raised to a level pre-determined by the Rules of Racing governing particular types of race. For example, most National Hunt races, with the principal exception of those over extreme distances, demand a top weight of at least 11 stone 10 pounds. If, after the overnight stage, the highest remaining horse was originally allotted 11st 5lb, his weight will be increased by 5lb to bring him up to the required 11st 10lb. All those under him will be raised correspondingly by 5lb, the *relative* weights remaining the same.

The maximum weight in Flat racing also varies from race to race, usually between 10st 0lb and 9st 7lb. The principle of raising the weights remains exactly the same: as the higher weighted horses drop out, so those below them are brought up the handicap. Should a handicap attract too many runners for safety, elimination starts at the bottom of the handicap and works upwards. The least talented runners, on paper at least, are the most vulnerable.

An owner planning a campaign in handicaps needs to be aware of his horse's position in the weights relative to the safety limit. You will often hear trainers say: 'Mine needs five to come out before he can run', meaning at least five of those above him must withdraw for that horse to be guaranteed a run. In that position, an owner is entirely at the mercy of circumstance. Others may be equally keen to contest the race, so the number of declarations leaves you out in the cold. There is nothing you can do about individual races, but, if your horse is in danger of losing one opportunity, investigate other races as a possible back-up.

Equally, by studying the weights in advance you will know if your horse is certain to run. If he is, and that is his intended target, there is little point wasting other entries.

As handicaps have a pre-arranged top-weight, so they equally have an agreed bottom weight. National Hunt horses do not carry below 10st 0lb and Flat horses have a minimum 7st 7lb, both excluding riders' allowances. It should be remembered that for a horse to be eliminated from a handicap it does not have to be less than the minimum weight, only beneath the safety limit wherever that is drawn.

The long handicap

The fixed bottom weight brings with it the question of the 'long handicap', which can bemuse even quite experienced race watchers. Although each race has its bottom level, the handicappers allot weight below that level as a true reflection of horses' ability. It is not uncommon to see, for example, a horse allotted 6st 13lb in a Flat handicap, or 9st 3lb in a National Hunt handicap. Although neither will be allowed to carry that weight (both will be raised to the minimum of their respective codes), it shows that the handicapper feels both horses are only moderate judged by the standards of that particular race.

The principle of long handicaps as it applies to entries is important, both from an ownership and betting point of view. When a horse is carrying significantly more than its long handicap weight, it is lumbered with a major disadvantage. The horse is meeting the opposition on unfavourable terms even before the race begins. In our example, the Flat runner has an 8lb 'penalty' and the jumper 11lb.

Running a horse with more than its allotted weight (from out of the handicap) is bad practice and should be discouraged. Horses do occasionally win from out of the handicap, sometimes because they are improving and are ahead of the handicapper's assessment of their ability, and sometimes from sheer chance. But there is simply no point in presenting your rivals with an advantage, even one of a couple of pounds. Winning races is hard enough without letting everybody else have a head start. In the majority of cases, if a horse runs from out of the handicap it is a sign that it is being run out of its class. That is bad for owners, who are wasting money on entry fees for the wrong races, and for punters, who are backing horses which have a very stiff task at the prevailing weights.

It is an intriguing exercise, especially for new owners, to watch patterns of entry. Keep an eye on the way races change from the five-day stage to the overnight stage, how the weights are adjusted and just how many horses do run from out of the handicap. You will soon begin to get the feel of which horses are being given a realistic chance of winning, and which are not. The lessons can be applied to making the most of your own horse, and saving money as you learn from other people's misjudgements.

Early-closing races

Although the five-day system applies to the overwhelming majority of races in the calendar, many of the top races under both codes close much earlier. The Derby closes about three months before it is run on the first Wednesday in June, while the Grand National closes more than two months before the great spectacle in early April. A number of valuable Flat and jump handicaps also close well in advance, particularly the races which traditionally attract strong betting interest. The Cambridgeshire and the Cesarewitch, Newmarket's Autumn Double, and the Hennessy Gold Cup Chase at Newbury are good examples. Even in early closing races, however, entries must be confirmed at the five-day stage.

Early closing races do not, however, appeal to everyone. Many trainers are critical of a system which forces them to make judgements on a horse's ability too far in advance. A major debate centres on several of the season's top two-year-old races in October, entries for which close fully six months in advance.

Trainers ask: How can we possibly know which will be our best horses before we have even given them any serious work? There is, however, the loophole of the supplementary entry, but available only at a price. For a proportion of those races which close very early, owners may enter their horses about two weeks before the race, but at a far greater cost than by progressing through the usual forfeit stages.

The Cheveley Park Stakes at Newmarket, confined to two-year-old fillies, is one such race to offer this facility, which was adroitly capitalised on in 1989. Although a late entry cost £10,000, several trainers took up the option, including David Elsworth, who provided the winner, Dead Certain. In the 1990 Irish Derby, Salsabil and Deploy, who finished first and second, were each supplemented at a cost of Ir£60,000.

There is a lot to be said for using the supplementary entry. If the horse is entered, the chances are it has already shown plenty of ability and has clear prospects of victory. It is a growing trend among even the wealthiest owners to stop entering *en masse*, preferring instead to wait for the supplementary stage when they know precisely the strength of their challenge. There is the further consideration that if a horse is good enough to warrant a supplementary entry, it has probably covered the extra cost in prize-money already won.

As a historical footnote, the five-day system superseded the old arrangement by which horses were, in most instances, entered initially about three weeks before the race and confirmed at what was then the four-day stage. The overnight stage remains the same. But that was heavy on entries as trainers tended to adopt a scattergun policy and enter horses all over the place without giving any real thought to a horse's probable target.

With the five-day method, the assumption is that a trainer should know at five days' notice whether a horse is likely to be fit to run in a given race. Entries are therefore fewer as they are probable, rather than possible, runners. Some trainers have taken longer than others to absorb the basic message of being more selective. If your trainer is continuing to put your horse in everywhere only for it to miss the majority of those engagements, tell him you would appreciate greater discrimination in the way he spends your money.

8: The financing of races

During 1989 owners contributed a total of some £10 million under both codes, around 25 per cent of the total prize-money on offer. As well as providing racing's raw material – the horse – the owner also puts up a sizeable proportion of the money he is seeking to win.

Prize-money comes principally from three other sources: the Horserace Betting Levy Board (informally known as the Levy Board), sponsorship and the individual racecourse executives.

The Levy Board is the keeper of racing's purse-strings. It was established in 1961 to assess and collect a levy from bookmakers and the Horserace Totalisator Board (the Tote), and apply that money to the improvement of breeds of horses, veterinary science and education and the improvement of racing.

The levy on off-course turnover is currently just under one pence per £, the scale of the levy being reviewed annually in discussions between the Board and bookmakers' representatives. Should mutual agreement not be reached, the matter goes before the Home Secretary who makes the final decisions. On-course bookmakers also make a small contribution to the levy.

The levy, although a charge on bookmakers, is collected from the punter. Bookmakers generally charge 10 per cent deduction on stakes or on 'returns' to cover the 8 per cent Betting Duty, the levy and other costs.

Trying to balance the arguments presented by both sides is a brain-wrenching business. In simple terms, the Levy Board feels the bookmakers should contribute more. The bookmakers argue they already have their hands deep enough in their pockets, although the cynic would suggest that the pockets belong to the punter. The Board and the bookmakers do, in fact, share a common aim: the greater the turnover, the greater the levy. The introduction of Satellite Information Services (SIS), which televises racing in betting shops, has had a dramatic effect for both parties. Indeed, figures suggest that its introduction has sparked nothing less than a betting boom, with turnover up by some 33 per cent in the financial years 1988–89 and 1989–90.

Having collected the levy, which was some £36 million for 1989–90, the Board then sets about allocating it. The distribution covers prize-money, loans to racecourses to improve facilities, grants to various veterinary organisations, and a plethora of other recipients which maintain the quality and integrity of racing. The policy on prize-money is to support where possible what are described as the lower-tier races.

They include lower-grade handicaps and maiden races on the Flat, maiden and novice hurdles over jumps, and selling and claiming races under both codes. The aim is to try to achieve the most for the horses which occupy the lower rungs of racing's ladder. In short, the vast majority.

Sponsorship has become an increasingly important contributor to racing's finances. Yet its seal of ultimate approval came only during the Eighties when a cash crisis at the Levy Board forced the Jockey Club to open the five Flat racing Classics to commercial sponsorship. Despite the apoplectic opposition of some of the Club's more ostrich-headed members, outside funding was approved, and there is no evidence the quintet has come to any harm by its marriage to Mammon. At all levels of the sport, sponsorship is now an accepted fact of life. There is a great symbiotic relationship between course and sponsor: the sponsor brings in welcome finance, and the course provides its expertise in giving the sponsor's guests a good day out.

There is, however, one notable pocket of resistance to spon-

The financing of races

sorship, despite the battalions of change battering at the gates: Royal Ascot. The Ascot authority refuses to allow sponsorship during its four-day meeting in June, which draws the finest collection of Thoroughbreds assembled in one place during the Flat season. At a time when the industry is pressing for more money, Ascot's attitude smacks of blinkered self-interest. Sanctioning sponsorship, and there would be no shortage of applicants, would release funds much needed by those less insulated from the harsher facts of economic life.

Racecourses are the smallest subscribers. This is not out of calculated parsimony, but many courses have, in the past, struggled to make worthwhile profits. Their contribution must come from operating profits, and when they are slim other sources must play a greater part.

By knitting these four strands together, courses construct a financial framework for individual races. The Levy Board grant and the course's own contribution are the two main elements. They will determine the owners' contribution through entry fees. Also, not every race will be sponsored, so that particular input cannot be guaranteed.

In considering an individual race, the course will put together the Levy Board money and its own contribution, adding sponsorship money where applicable, to come up with an 'added value'. That means the sum will be added to owners' entry fees to form the total prize-money. If the added value is £3,000, the entry fee will, in most cases, be one per cent of that value – £30 in this instance. Multiply the number of entries by £30, add the total to the £3,000 already accounted for, and you have the prize-money for that race. Although this is a simplified example, it serves to illustrate the parts played by the various inputs.

The distribution of prize-money changes according to the category of race and the number of places which command a return. Some races have prize-money for the first three only, some the first four, and others, usually big races, can award prizes down to sixth place. It is governed by a complex set of formulae laid down in the Rules of Racing, but in general owners can expect between 45 and 50 per cent of the prize pool.

Confusion often arises between the owner's share and the

penalty value, which are always different. The penalty value is the value upon which penalties for subsequent races are based. It is that part of the prize pool which goes to the winner and its connections, but is higher than the owner's share because that share does not include any element of the jockey's or trainer's percentages, and other deductions which may be made.

Breakdown of 1989 prize-money

Flat

Owners	£7,359,373
Sponsors	£5,876,951
Levy Board	£9,934,418
Racecourses	£4,362,394
Total	£27,533,136

National Hunt

Owners	£2,384,427
Sponsors	£2,476,084
Levy Board	£6,952,825
Racecourses	£1,211,599
Total	£13,024,935

Reproduced by courtesy of the Jockey Club

9: Jockeys

The jockey has the least contact with the horse, yet the few minutes they are together can determine victory and defeat. A good jockey rarely loses races he should have won. Sometimes, more infrequently, he may win races he should, by rights, have lost. A moment's error of judgement can be very expensive. Days, weeks and months of a horse's preparation can be rendered worthless in a fraction of a second. 'Good horses make good jockeys' runs the old adage. True enough, and no jockey on earth can win without the horse. But the best jockeys coax the maximum from their mounts.

Pat Eddery and Steve Cauthen on the Flat, and Peter Scudamore and Richard Dunwoody over jumps are names that always spring to mind. Booking jockeys, probably more than anything else in racing, is about fashion. Yet there are many highly competent riders around who can win if the horse is good enough. Racing is full of jockeys searching for that one elusive horse to bring them wider recognition.

All trainers have their favoured jockeys. Assuming your trainer does not employ a stable rider (if he does, the decision will be ready-made), he will try to engage whichever of his preferred jockeys is available. Jockeys are often a sore point between trainers and owners: an owner demands one rider, the trainer stoutly defends his choice, arguments follow. Trainers can be fiercely loyal, particularly over stable jockeys, and many a behind-the-scenes trial of strength has been fought between owner and trainer. If an owner is strongly opposed to a particular jockey, the trainer should respect the view and try to accommodate him.

Most owners, especially newcomers, revel in the idea of having Eddery or Scudamore riding for them. Unless your trainer has a prior claim on the top jockeys, the probability of that happening is directly dependent on your horse's chance of winning.

The leading riders, or more precisely their agents, must be businesslike. A top jockey is a highly saleable commodity, and his agent will only commit him to rides which he believes have good prospects of success. If your horse is not thought likely to win, the jockey will look elsewhere.

After riding in a race, a jockey should be able to tell you something you did not already know: it would prefer a longer distance, it did not like the ground, blinkers would help it to concentrate, and so on. The jockey is your only contact with the horse in its racing element. It is as much his duty to be informative as to try to win.

Riding fees are agreed by negotiation between the Jockeys' Association and the Racehorse Owners' Association. If mutual agreement cannot be reached, the stewards of the Jockey Club will be asked to mediate. That, however, is a course both parties try to avoid. The new rates are introduced for the opening of the National Hunt season, applicable to both Flat and jump jockeys from that time.

The Flat jockey's fee is £49.00 per ride, and the jump jockey's £66.80. To that is added 15 per cent VAT (applicable to only a relatively small number under both codes), and a contribution to the Professional Riders' Insurance Scheme of 10 per cent for Flat jockeys (£4.90) and 12½ per cent for jump jockeys (£8.35). Assuming a jockey is registered for VAT, the total cost would be £61.25 on the Flat and £85.17 over jumps.

Under the Professional Riders' Insurance Scheme (PRIS), jockeys are graded from one to six depending on how many rides they have each season. They are repaid, when injured, commensurate with their grading when injured. Thus, a top

Jockeys

jockey in grade one would receive more than a less fashionable rider in grade six. The Injured Jockeys' Fund, although it has a higher profile than the PRIS, is not funded by direct contribution but relies on public support. Its greetings cards are a regular feature of racing's Christmas.

The fees cover all categories of jockeys. On the Flat, a full jockey will retain all of the fee. An apprentice must equally share his fee and earnings with his master, the trainer to whom he is apprenticed. The theory is that the apprentice repays the time and effort a trainer has put in on his behalf, although some trainers are considerably more skilled and sympathetic in their development of apprentices than others.

The situation is more complex for conditional riders over jumps, where the fee and earnings situation depends on the experience of the rider. However, whatever the status of the jockey, the fee will not vary much from the basic level.

Until an amateur rider has had 75 rides against professionals, excluding those on family-owned horses, the owner does not have to pay a riding fee. Even then, a fee is only payable if the amateur is competing against professionals, and not on a family-owned runner. No fees would be payable in amateur riders' races under either code. Amateurs themselves receive no riding fee but, when a fee is applicable (using the laid-down scale), it goes to the Jockey Club for distribution within racing.

In addition to riding fees, jockeys receive a percentage of the prize-money of win and place mounts. The calculations are intricate and differ according to the type of race. Also, jockeys who ride big-race winners, particularly colts, often secure a share of the horse when it retires to stud.

To encourage trainers to use apprentice and conditional riders, there is a fixed scale of weight allowances which less experienced riders may claim. Both codes divide claims into 7lb, 5lb or 3lb, depending on numbers of winners ridden. On the Flat, an apprentice claims 7lb until he has ridden 10 winners, 5lb up to 50, and 3lb up to 75, when the allowance disappears. Over jumps, it is 7lb up to 15 winners, 5lb up to 25, and 3lb up to 40. The allowances are bound to a set time scale. On the Flat, an apprenticeship ends, regardless of the number of winners, at the age of 24. He is no longer allowed to claim, or ride in apprentice races. Over jumps, a conditional rider loses his claim at 25, but can hold a conditional licence for a further three months.

There are limitations to the races in which allowances may be claimed. Riders can claim in almost all handicaps (the Grand National is a notable exception) but are prevented from doing so in the valuable conditions races.

Whether to employ a claiming rider is dependent on the individual jockey. The more polished can be excellent value for their allowance. They reduce the horse's weight, but, more importantly, have sufficient ability to deliver a competent ride despite their apparent inexperience. But giving an apprentice the ride for the sole reason of taking off some weight is short-sighted. An apprentice may claim 7lb, yet he may so lack any skill that even a 14lb allowance would not compensate. The right claimer can be a sound investment, but the wrong one may harm your chances of success.

The apprentice versus full-jockey debate must also consider the horse. Some horses are easy to handle, and will do their best for the experienced jockey, apprentice and amateur alike. Others, however, can be tricky rides, best matched with greater experience. A horse can be lazy during a race, requiring plenty of pushing and shoving. He may have to be held up to the last second before making his challenge. Or he may be a poor jumper who must be presented properly at his fences. For those horses which require that extra degree of skill and strength, a full-jockey is the best answer.

A trainer would need a very good reason to put up an apprentice in a race in which he cannot exercise his right to claim. If he is unable to claim, he is being penalised for his inexperience. In such circumstances, it is far better to use an established jockey.

10: A day at the races

The racecourse captures the essence of ownership. The moment of truth has arrived, and the hours of dreaming, planning and preparing are about to be put to the test. But, above all, a day at the races should be fun. Set out to enjoy yourself, to revel in the occasion of seeing your colours carried, to hear the commentator calling your horse's name. To go in the expectation of success is to invite disappointment; go instead to enjoy the day, and regard winning as a glorious bonus.

The trainer should be there to guide you. His presence is part of your day, to offer encouragement, congratulation, commiseration or a large drink to soothe the nerves. This is one area in which the smaller trainer does come up trumps. He is much more likely to go racing with his owners, fostering a greater team spirit between himself and the owners. The top trainers tend to be more guilty of staying away, although it should be said that the leading owners, who account for a large proportion of those trainers' patronage, are often absent themselves.

The owner is advised to make his own arrangements to secure badges for admission, which should be collected at the entrance to the racecourse. The recommended minimum quota per horse is two, regardless of the category of ownership, and four for any form of multiple ownership, that is, partnerships, companies and so on, granted prior application for the additional two. Where more than four people are concerned, it is up to the individuals to work out who will take the badges. Those who miss out on one occasion should go to the top of the list for the next.

If you arrive at the course to be told that your tickets have been given to someone pretending to be you (not an uncommon ruse among unscrupulous racegoers trying to get in for nothing), do not be fobbed off. It is the racecourse's responsibility, not yours, to check identification and make sure it is giving tickets to the right person. If the gate official hands out badges injudiciously, that is his responsibility. But the reverse is also true. If you have failed to make adequate provision for badges, it is unfair to berate the gateman when he had no idea you were coming.

It should be stressed that badges are available only to owners with a runner at that meeting. An ROA member's sticker should, however, be sufficient to gain access to the owners' car park, even if you are not actively involved in the day's racing. Should you be fortunate enough to have a runner at one of the big meetings such as Royal Ascot, Cheltenham or Liverpool, contact the course to ascertain whether any special badges are required. This is particularly true of car parking, as large crowds mean space is at a premium.

Some racecourses can be generous in their interpretation of the recommended badges. Given sufficient notice, they may well allow an owner in excess of the minimum. Others, sadly, can be downright bad. Trying to make contact is nightmarish – telephones unanswered or constantly engaged, badges grudgingly issued, staff unhelpful (even at times verging on the belligerent).

The owner will also quickly realise that at most courses his badge offers little more than admission. Some courses do provide an owners' and trainers' bar, but by no means all. Nor can you expect a reserved viewing area to watch the race unhindered. If an owner chooses to visit the paddock, he will need a turn of foot not far removed from that of his horse if he is to find a good position in the stands. Owners do more than anybody to keep racing going, and it is not unreasonable to expect racecourses to show them some consideration.

Go equipped with a copy of *The Sporting Life* for an in-depth assessment of the meeting, or even take your own daily newspaper. Racecards are, all too often, sadly lacking in information. Many carry only the bare list of runners and colours, without up-to-date riding arrangements or a description of the horse's form.

Once inside, you will be able to scout around for a bar or buffet to have a drink or something to eat. Like everything else, catering facilities vary tremendously from course to course. Racecourse catering is a subject always guaranteed to raise the blood pressure. Its fiercest critics, and there is no shortage of them, would say it ranges from the atrocious to the simply adequate. Simple, good-quality fare at reasonable prices is what the race-goer wants, but only infrequently finds.

The business of the day will begin with the declaration of your horse and jockey 45 minutes before the off-time. Jockeys do sometimes have to be changed. If you are in an early race, he could be delayed by traffic, or be injured in a previous race. Injury will be a greater factor in National Hunt racing, where falls are a way of life. Indeed, it is not uncommon for a rider with a fancied mount in a big race to give up his previous rides that day to avoid injury.

Making a late substitution can be unfortunate, particularly if the intended rider gets on well with the horse. However, replacements are always available and it is up to the trainer or his representative to secure the best alternative.

The jockey will weigh out with his saddle, which will contain lead to make up the difference if a rider does not reach the horse's allotted weight naturally. The trainer then takes the saddle to put on the horse, which is then ready to make its appearance in the paddock.

The horses enter the paddock about 20 minutes before the 'off', to give everybody time to cast an eye over them. If you have not already joined your trainer, now is the time to walk into the paddock and meet him there.

The jockey will join you, mostly to exchange a few pleasantries before he mounts. Any serious discussion of the horse's chance and riding instructions will have taken place between trainer and jockey beforehand. If you have confidence in the jockey, there is no point tying him down with reams of instructions. Apart from any foibles the horse may have, such as needing to be brought with a late run, it is best to let the jockey ride the race as he sees fit. If the unexpected occurs, and the chances are that it will, he needs the freedom to make an instant decision.

As the horse and rider make their way to the start, now is the time to place your bet, if you have not already done so. Race-course betting is divided between the bookmakers and the Tote. The bookmakers are lined up in rows, their boards displaying the current odds about the horses. The bookmakers are synonymous with a day's racing. The shouting of the odds, the white-gloved tic-tacs relaying changes in the betting, the backers dodging back and forth to obtain the best odds available for their choice.

Even those most committed to the abolition of off-course bookmakers in favour of a Tote monopoly tend to admit bookmakers help bring a race meeting to life. However much we envy the superior financial standing of some overseas racing, those who have been racing abroad will have noted the lack of atmosphere without bookmakers.

The on-course bookmakers do offer other advantages. There is the opportunity to try to get the best odds for your fancy. Bookmakers do not offer uniform prices, so the backer can, by walking up and down the rows, see which of the bookmakers are advertising the biggest odds. Also, there is no tax on on-course bets, a considerable advantage for those used to suffering 10 per cent deductions in betting shops. When the bet has been struck, the bookmaker issues a numbered ticket as a record. This is then presented for payment if the bet is a winner.

The alternative is to bet with the Tote. This is pool betting, with the pool, after deductions, being divided between the numbers of winning tickets. You can bet win and place (the equivalent of each-way), place only or attempt to forecast the first two, in either order, with a dual-forecast. The major meetings operate a Jackpot pool, in which backers must select the winners of the first six races. A Placepot pool, forecasting placed horses in the first six races, is available at all meetings.

The principal difference between betting with bookmakers and the Tote is that a bet with a bookmaker is struck at a definite price, so the backer knows exactly where he stands. With the

A day at the races

Tote, a winning bet is paid at the returned dividend calculated after the start of the race when all bets are in. Although the Tote has made many helpful innovations in recent years (mainly as a result of computer technology), such as up-to-the-moment Tote odds displayed on video screens, there will always be an element of uncertainty for the backer.

After the race, the stewards may call an enquiry if there is evidence of interference, or a jockey can lodge an objection if he feels he was unfairly hampered by another horse. For the stewards to change the placings they must be satisfied, in a case in which they consider the interference was accidental, that the horse causing the interference improved his placing because of it. If the interference was caused by careless riding, the horse causing the interference will be placed behind the horse with which it interfered. In extreme cases, the offender could be disqualified altogether, and its jockey suspended. An objection must be accompanied by a deposit, which may not be returned if the objection is held to be frivolous.

If a horse's connections are dissatisfied with the decision of the racecourse stewards, often referred to as the 'local stewards', they may appeal to the Jockey Club in London to reconsider the decision. Owners generally accept the verdict of the local stewards, but an appeal to the Jockey Club is often pursued by riders who believe a suspension to have been too harsh.

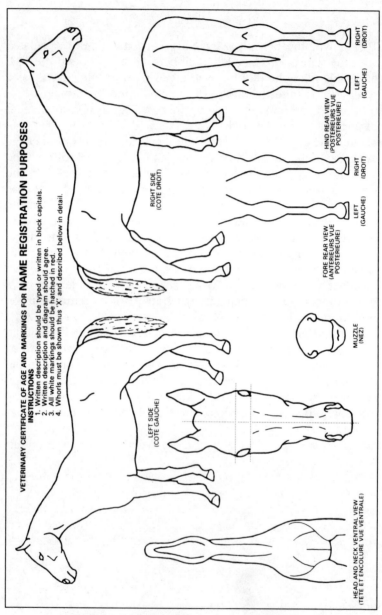

*Markings diagram from a racehorse passport
(reproduced by courtesy of the Jockey Club)*

112

11: The vet

A veterinary surgeon is, like a doctor in our lives, indispensable to the horse. His duties vary from the life-saving to the relatively mundane chores of vaccination and the completing of a horse's passport. He is also an integral part of the training regime, often working closely with the trainer on the general health of the stable.

Trainers vary in their willingness to call upon a vet's assistance, and it is impossible to be completely objective about a particular trainer's attitude. What one person may view as being over-cautious, a trainer could justify as being prudent. Another trainer's apparently cavalier outlook of rarely resorting to veterinary treatment may simply be a belief that he, the trainer, is thoroughly capable of judging his horses' well-being.

There are no hard and fast rules. Provided concern for the horses' welfare remains beyond reproach, there is no reason to feel that one viewpoint is necessarily better than the other.

Vaccinations
Not all decisions regarding veterinary treatment are left to individual discretion. The Rules of Racing demand that horses be vaccinated and set down prescribed time scales for primary injections and boosters. The Jockey Club requires only that a

horse be vaccinated against equine flu, although in many cases additional protection is administered. A tetanus vaccine is usually given, generally incorporated into the flu shot.

A horse should be given primary injections not less than 21 and not more than 92 days apart. Boosters must then be given between 150 and 215 days after the second primary. The programme then goes on to annual boosters. A horse cannot race until seven days (reduced from 10 during 1990) after its latest injection. A booster is less severe than the primary and will usually have few side-effects, although it is recommended for horses to be given only light exercise after vaccination.

Most horses are vaccinated before they reach the sales ring as yearlings. They would be vaccinated as foals and yearlings on the stud from which they come, and the vaccinations noted on the Foal Identification Certificate. The horse is then presented for sale with those vaccinations recorded.

The rules dictate that boosters be administered within a calendar year so treatment revolves around the same period each year. Christmas Eve is particularly popular with the Flat racing brigade. Not only does it allow plenty of time before the onset of the traditional season in March, but it also gives trainers a marvellous excuse for having greatly reduced exercise on Christmas Day and Boxing Day.

Vaccination is not as time-consuming as the observer may believe. One leading Newmarket vet reckons to vaccinate a 100-strong stable in about an hour and a half given sound organisation beforehand.

National Hunt horses, who are working during the winter, have to be vaccinated to a different time-scale. Vets try to organise the jumpers into a system where they are vaccinated while at grass during the summer before they come back into training in the autumn.

The vaccination framework is not simply a matter of regulations. It is designed to protect the health of the horse population at large. During 1989, equine flu, which spreads like wildfire, swept through Newmarket. However, vaccination ensured that, even if horses caught the infection, its effects were short-lived. Early fears that race fields would be greatly reduced proved unfounded as horses were able to shake off the illness in weeks rather than months.

Meetings between the various international veterinary bodies have discussed the implications of compulsorily increasing the vaccinations to every six months rather than annually, but the issue remains unresolved. The wild card is the efficacy of vaccines. Research into equine flu, and the vaccines used to combat it, is continuing all the time. Some authorities, including the Jockey Club, advise six-monthly boosters, but the general feeling is that it would be self-defeating to introduce rules which may be obsolete in a few years. Vaccines are almost sure to improve to the point where the annual injection will provide sufficient protection.

Passports

The vet's other staple task is dealing with a horse's passport. A passport is required once the horse is named so, when a name has been finalised, the trainer will ask his vet to note the horse's markings on the naming form.

Date of birth, colour, sire and dam must be recorded, and the form also shows silhouettes of various aspects of the horse (right side, left side, fore- and hind-legs and so on) on which the vet marks distinguishing features. White hair, which may, for example, appear as socks or as a blaze on the forehead, is the most common, although other features are commonly recorded. Whorls (points where the hair grows in circles and common to all horses), 'Prophet's thumbmarks' (indentations in the muscle, usually on the neck), and scars will also be included. Indeed, anything which helps to distinguish one horse from another should be noted and described.

The markings are the basis of the passport. The original form is retained by Weatherbys as a master copy. From the information supplied, a duplicate is produced which goes into the passport, produced by Weatherbys, and sent to the trainer. Vaccinations are also certified on the passport.

Markings are generally held to be a safe way of accurately identifying a particular horse. The Jockey Club's view is that each horse has three characteristics which make it unique, although some countries do use technology, rather than sole reliance on the human eye. Many racing authorities in the United States, for example, tattoo horses with an indelible number which is their identification for life.

The marking system, although primarily based on human judgement, is now backed by a blood-typing programme administered by Weatherbys and conducted by the Animal Health Trust in Newmarket. A minimum of a month after birth, foals are sampled to prove that their blood type is consistent with their parentage. In some ways similar to genetic finger-printing, blood-typing works by exclusion. It can tell when a horse does not have its supposed parentage and demonstrates that it could be the product of a particular mating.

Stallions and broodmares, horses which are likely to have a continuing effect on the breed, are blood-typed at the end of their racing careers to make certain they are, in fact, who we think they are. Mix-ups, though uncommon, can and do happen. A celebrated case during the Eighties concerned the King George VI & Queen Elizabeth Diamond Stakes winner Kalaglow, who was found to be out of the mare Rossitor rather than Aglow as had previously been thought. It was an important discovery. Although his 'new' pedigree could have no effect on his racing record, it changed how breeders viewed Kalaglow the stallion. By changing his female line, projections of his success at stud also have to be reconsidered. Aglow's legacy does, however, survive in the second half of Kalaglow's name.

A more recent example came to light during a court case early in 1990. The connections of Fondu were awarded £50,000 damages when it transpired that the horse was out of a different, and less attractive, dam to the one they had supposed. Blood-typing established the horse's rightful parentage.

The passport is central to the horse's racing career because it must always accompany the horse. Jockey Club veterinary officers check the passport the first time a horse runs, and randomly after that. The system is not truly random, however, because the Jockey Club tries to check an individual passport once each season. Passport irregularities can result in a fine or, even worse, the horse could be prevented from running.

The vet

Problem areas

Aside from vaccinations and passports, a vet's greatest contact with a stable is likely to be in dealing with lameness and respiratory diseases.

Lameness has been identified by a series of surveys as the major source of wastage in racing stables. From a vet's point of view, it is a notably time-consuming ailment. To ascertain the extent of the damage, X-rays are usually needed. In the case of a suspected complicated injury, that in turn may necessitate the horse being brought to a powerful standing machine rather than examination by portable X-ray.

The types of injury will vary in different groups of horses. Young horses are susceptible to joint and bone problems resulting from the demands of training before their skeletons mature. Older horses, particularly steeplechasers, are more prone to tendon problems brought on by a combination of general wear and tear and the specific requirements of jumping fences. Tendon injuries, in any category, are particularly awkward, not least because of the lack of a proven, successful treatment. There is always the danger that they will recur, and any owner considering buying a horse which has had tendon difficulties should be especially wary.

The racehorse, in common with any athlete, will be at risk from being subjected to a controlled and often rigorous training and racing regime. By pushing a body, human or equine, to its limits, weaknesses are exposed. Racing is built on speed. Its greatest horses, and therefore those seen as most suitable for stud purposes, are those which have run fastest, not those which demonstrated their durability. One of racing's most enduring arguments suggests that breeders should place greater emphasis on the proven soundness of horses retiring to stud. By breeding from them, the theory goes, we will produce harder-wearing individuals. But fashion rules – speed is king and likely to remain so.

As well as physical defects, there is also the dreaded 'virus', which is guaranteed to give trainers sleepless nights. It is especially worrisome as it threatens the stable as a whole. In fact, 'the virus' is a misnomer because the terminology suggests there is only one. There are a whole series of viral infections and trainers are apt to use the term as a blanket heading for any affliction which happens to hit the yard.

But however viral infection manifests itself, it is a thoroughly unwelcome visitor. Trainers are usually first aware of a problem through horses having high temperatures and runny noses. Once the illness has been confirmed, either by veterinary diagnosis or a trainer simply recognising the symptoms, the best cure is time. Horses should not be subjected to the greatest stresses of training while they are ill. Recovery is made more unpredictable by the effects lingering after the obvious signs of illness have gone. Horses may be eating normally and to all intents and purposes be back to their best, yet not reproducing their form on the track.

Rates of recovery will also vary from stable to stable. Two trainers may say they have the virus but it does not automatically follow that both will take the same time to be back in business. The strains are not equally debilitating, and recovery will also be influenced by the circumstances of an individual yard. The degree of fitness of the horses, the way the outbreak was handled and the quality of hygiene in the stable are factors which help or hinder the return to full health.

A parallel problem with viral infection is the difficulty of protection through vaccination. There is not, as yet, a demonstrably effective viral vaccine, although widespread research is being conducted.

Controlling, let alone eradicating, viral problems is a massive task. Apart from the limitations of vaccination, the growth of international racing has thrown together more and more horses in close proximity, increasing the likelihood of disease spreading. Racing stables are like boarding schools. When a large group is assembled from a wide range of sources, the prospect of infection being introduced grows significantly. Those horses, or pupils, with no immunity to a particular illness are automatically at risk.

One area in which science, as applied to racing, has become widely used is in blood-testing. Martin Pipe, the outstandingly successful National Hunt trainer, is probably the most famous exponent of the art. Pipe has his own laboratory at his Wellington stables and will not run a horse if he feels the blood test shows a horse is not 100 per cent. 'It takes the guesswork out of training,' he says, and his record makes it difficult to argue the point.

However, Pipe's system is built on regular testing, and therein lies its greatest usefulness. By monitoring horses on a regular basis, it is possible to detect trends within the stable and therefore help a trainer to run his horses when he knows them to be in peak condition. To borrow another of Pipe's sayings, 'It won't tell you if a horse is going to win but it will give you a good idea if it isn't.'

For most trainers, who would not use blood testing so regularly, it is a useful device if horses are unwell. As an assessor of fitness, its importance is rather more debatable. It is not guaranteed to show up everything which contributes to a horse running badly, because by no means all of them affect the blood. It is, however, valuable, not least psychologically, as the last piece in the jigsaw. A horse may look well, be working well and be ready to run in a race in which it has an oustanding chance. A satisfactory blood test may reveal what, in the trainer's eyes, is the final piece of information about the horse's chance.

While science and veterinary medicine can combine to assist sound health, there remains the ever-present threats of potential physical flaws and lurking infection. With those in mind, an owner is being naive if he believes that he has in his possession a machine so reliable it will only ever require minor maintenance here and there. It is, literally, the nature of the beast that things can go disastrously and expensively wrong. That eventuality, depressing though it is, can never be discounted.

12: Insurance

For horses bought at auction, bloodstock insurance is instituted as 'fall-of-the-hammer insurance'. By definition, it becomes effective when the auctioneer's hammer falls, that is, at the point of sale, when the buyer becomes legally responsible for the horse. The owner should then, if he has not done so previously, approach a recognised broker specialising in bloodstock insurance and take out cover which becomes effective immediately. The average policy is designed to cover all risks of mortality, that is, death by accident, sickness or disease. That basic framework will usually apply to colts and fillies, yearlings or horses in training. Should you buy an in-foal broodmare, it is also possible to insure the unborn foal, also under the fall-of-the-hammer system.

Not all owners agree on the necessity of being insured. The conditions are highly specific and, in most circumstances, the basic policy will not cover such eventualities as injury which is non-fatal but nevertheless ends a horse's career.

With that limitation in mind, loss-of-use cover, which applies when a horse cannot be used for the purpose for which it was intended, can be arranged. However, it is done very much on an individual basis and is also considerably more expensive. The theory is appealing, but expect the premiums to rise towards 8 per cent of the insured sum, almost double the usual rate on the Flat.

Insurance

The requirements are also more searching. Most significantly, a horse has to be proven in absolutely A1 condition by a special veterinary report, similar to an in-depth surveyor's report on a property. A simple veterinary certification, confirming that the horse is fit for insurance purposes, is not enough. Even then there are grey areas. If a horse is injured badly enough to prevent it fulfilling its potential but not severely enough to stop it racing again, a claim will not be paid. The nub of a loss-of-use policy is that a horse must not be able to perform: if a horse can race, whether it wins or not is of no consequence. It has returned to the course and therefore fulfilled its use. Its ability is not the question at issue.

The loss-of-use policy is, however, not very popular. The higher premiums deter owners and the insurance companies generally dislike it because of the high risk. Indeed, one leading bloodstock insurance company with some 4,000 clients has just 50 loss-of-use policies on Thoroughbreds on its books.

If a horse is bought privately, the owner can telephone a broker personally, or arrange for his trainer to initiate cover on his behalf. The insurance company will log the day and time at which the policy becomes effective, because a good deal of insurance is effected at short notice. An owner may, for example, have bought a horse with engagements in the next day or two and need it insured for those races.

The rate for Flat horses is usually around 4.25 per cent of the horse's value. If the horse is bought at public auction, the value is the fall-of-hammer price in pounds sterling. In that instance there is no need for a specific valuation, nor for a veterinary certificate.

However, even in circumstances where value appears to be cut-and-dried, there are possible pitfalls. For example, if a colt is gelded soon after purchase, there may be a reduction in its value following the loss of stallion potential. In that case, particularly with an expensive colt, the insurance company may ask the owner to reconsider the horse's valuation.

Although that type of revaluation is likely to apply mostly to owners in the upper reaches of the market, it underlines the basic principle that it is pointless for an owner to insure for more than the horse is worth. If a horse is bought privately, the same ground rules apply, although it is up to the owners to tell the insurers the purchase price.

Premiums in the National Hunt field are substantially higher because of the greater risks involved. A steeplechaser commands a basic rate of 12.5 per cent and hurdlers 8 per cent, although both figures may be discounted depending on, for example, how many horses an owner has, or just general negotiation. Even then, however, it is rare for a steeplechaser to be insured at less than 10.5 per cent.

Although Flat racers, steeplechasers and hurdlers are insured at different rates, a horse may quite easily compete in two or even all three disciplines. In its early days, a Flat horse will be confined to racing on the level, but, as it gets older, it may progress to alternating between Flat and National Hunt. The owner must then notify the insurers as to the change of plan. Likewise, a hurdler turning to steeplechasing must be insured at the higher rate. If an owner decides not to increase the premium, or just forgets, the insurers are not obliged to pay on the death of a steeplechaser which is insured for hurdling only. Companies differ and are reluctant to set hard-and-fast rules on how they would react to specific cases, but the burden is on the owner, or more probably a trainer acting for him. Ignorance or oversight is not a valid excuse.

Insuring horses bought out of a seller or claimer can be more difficult. If you are acting with a trainer, he may well have an arrangement with an insurer to guarantee cover from the moment the horse becomes your property. However, if you are on your own, you could be at risk until cover has been finalised, perhaps several hours later. It would be an unpleasant long-shot but horses can be injured just walking back to the box. Should that happen, insurers do not issue cover retrospectively.

If you are considering acquiring a horse this way, talk it over with your trainer first to be certain you are familiar with any problems which may arise.

Should you buy a horse directly from a trainer, you will only become liable for insurance premiums from the time of purchase. If the horse has been in the stable for three months previously, be careful that your bill does not include that time. You are not responsible for expenses incurred before you come on the scene.

As well as the possibility of reducing insurance, there is also the question of increasing it. If, for example, a well-bred filly wins her first race she will become a more attractive proposition. Cover can also be increased on the basis of home gallops, particularly two-year-olds. A youngster showing plenty of ability is potentially a valuable item and a likely candidate for a higher valuation. Insurers are perfectly happy to increase cover as long as it is justified.

The guidelines for bloodstock insurance are the same as for the domestic variety. Ask about the rates, how quickly the claims are paid, and do not be afraid to raise any queries you may have about the policy. In short, shop around.

13: Moving on

Nothing lasts for ever. One day horse and owner will part, it is just a question of when and how. When will be determined by personal circumstances. Do partners want to split up? Is there a profit to be realised? Are there losses to be cut? The scenarios are almost endless, less so the question of how. There are three principal methods of ending your involvement.

The stallion
To own a horse worthy of being retired as a stallion is to hit racing's jackpot. It could, theoretically, happen to anyone, but in practice it is usually the same people who hold the winning tickets. It is those who pay the top money at bloodstock sales, win the big races and then retire those winners to stud. The money realised by the sale of the stallion is re-cycled into buying yearlings, thus oiling the wheels of a self-perpetuating machine.

A stallion is usually syndicated in 40 shares. Its total value (which is then divided by 40 to give the share price) is dependent on a combination of its race record, pedigree and conformation. Ability is directly linked to the importance of the races a horse has won – a Derby winner will be a more lucrative proposition than the winner of a Group Three race.

Pedigree and conformation are assessed by the likelihood of

the stallion transmitting his most favourable traits to his offspring. Northern Dancer not only became a hugely influential sire in his own right, but produced top-class performers who, in turn, became successful stallions. A stallion by Northern Dancer would therefore be an attractive, and more valuable, proposition because of his pedigree. Breeders will also look closely at a horse's conformation for any physical shortcomings which may be passed on.

For any owner with a high-quality horse, his first decision on syndication will be based on how large a percentage of the horse he wants to retain. An owner with large breeding interests may, for example, wish to keep ten shares because he has a sufficient number of mares to justify that continuing investment. An owner with one or two mares may just keep a couple of shares.

However, an owner who has no interest in breeding, and no likelihood of using the stallion when it retires to stud, may decide not to have any shares in the horse. So, assuming a 40-share syndication, if an owner decides to keep 10 shares, only 30 will be available for general syndication. Most syndications are handled by bloodstock agencies.

The first stage of syndication is to find a stud at which the stallion will stand. The stud owner may also decide to take shares in the stallion, reducing further the number on offer. Many of the leading owners already own a stud as a base for their breeding operations. Once a stallion has found a home, potential share buyers will be circulated with the details.

The selling of a stallion raises other factors, namely the timing of the sale and the health of the market. A racehorse's value as a future stallion is highest when its reputation peaks. It is common for a horse to be syndicated as a stallion while it is still racing, usually in the wake of a big-race triumph, to maximise its appeal. Its value is also governed by the market's strength. Buyers' attitudes are clearly different when the market is depressed rather than buoyant.

Each share carries a nomination, that is, the right to send one mare each season to the stallion. If the shareholder does not wish to take up the nomination, he can sell it, although some syndicates stipulate it must first be offered to the other members of that syndicate.

There is a thriving market in the buying and selling of shares and nominations, more so in the case of nominations, which become available more frequently. Despite the 40-share syndicate, stallions may cover more than 40 mares each season, the additional income going towards the running expenses of the syndicate.

Breeding from mares

An owner intending to breed from his filly should have started to prepare the ground from the moment he bought her. If the filly has been purchased with an eye to breeding, it is important that her pedigree holds out the hope that she can produce horses with some ability. To buy a filly from a family with a poor winner-producing record is to load the dice against yourself. If the family as a whole is moderate, why should your filly be the exception?

The decision to breed should not be taken on the spur of the moment. It is no use buying a filly only to decide later that it may be worth having a go at breeding from her. You may have bought entirely the wrong filly in the first place.

Breeding your own racehorse is a romantic notion, but one which carries a hefty price tag. Even without the cost of a nomination to a stallion, expect to pay around £15,000 before your horse is even ready to race. You will also need plenty of patience. If you decide to have your mare covered in 1991, you will have the upkeep of the mare until she foals in 1992, and then have to pay for the mare and foal for that year. There are further keep charges when the foal becomes a yearling in 1993. Not until 1994 will the then two-year-old be ready to race.

That scenario portrays a trouble-free progression. On the downside, the mare could lose the foal, or the foal may have a physical defect which makes it unsuitable for racing. If you have bred to sell, buyers may simply take a dislike to it.

Lurking in the background is the spectre of over-production, breeding more yearlings than the market can absorb. Having jumped on the bandwagon of the bloodstock boom during the Eighties, breeders have found the market declining as supply outstrips demand.

Moving on

Anyone thinking of entering the market commercially should be aware of the very real financial dangers. For those who see it as the extension of a hobby it can be good, if expensive, fun.

Selling at auction

Here is proof of one of life's famous sayings: that buying and selling are two different things. The Mercedes you once bought has turned into a Lada! Figures confirm the impression. A survey by the Racehorse Owners' Association found that only 18 per cent of Flat-race yearlings bought in 1986 had, by 1989, been resold at a profit.

Any resale value your horse may have will be determined by the job it can continue to do. A racehorse sold to continue racing will be judged by the buyer's view of its potential to win races, either here or abroad. A steeplechaser may be bought to go point-to-pointing. A mare's value will be based on her breeding prospects. Even here, at the final stage of ownership, be realistic. If you submit a sow's ear, nobody will pay you the price of a silk purse.

To submit a horse for sale at auction, you will first have to decide upon a suitable sale. Assuming your horse has some miles on the clock, it will be a horses-in-training sale. A filly or mare may also be entered for a sale of breeding stock.

Sales companies advertise their upcoming sales to attract entries. When you decide upon your sale, write for an entry form to confirm your intention of selling there. Once your horse has been accepted, a fee, which varies according to the sale, is payable. Your horse must then be catalogued with its pedigree and details of winners in the family. Some sales will prepare the pedigree for you. Others may do, but prefer you to do it. Another company will tell you to do it yourself. By whichever method you are catalogued, the final responsibility is yours. The onus is on you to be sure that selling points have not been omitted.

You have the option of imposing a reserve, a minimum selling price, but there is no point if the horse is there to be sold. It is only worth considering such a course of action seriously if your horse has an obvious value and you do not want it to be sold for less than it is worth. Once the horse is sold, the auctioneers will charge a fee, usually 5 per cent of the sale price.

At some bloodstock auctions, it is a sad fact of life that horses sold at the very bottom price range, below 500 guineas, are in real danger of being bought for slaughter as horsemeat. If your horse has no obvious resale value, it could come to a gruesome end.

Ask your trainer what price he feels the horse will make. If his estimation is in the danger area, and you are concerned about the horse's fate, try to persuade the trainer to ask around for a home for it, not necessarily in racing. Horses with an equable temperament can find a new life show-jumping or eventing.

No matter how bad your horse, it is to be hoped he at least gave you some fun. Try to keep him out of harm's way.

14: Point-to-point racing

The growth of point-to-point racing has provided a worthy alternative to ownership in the mainstream. Point-to-points are steeplechases run by local hunts, often on land owned by farmers across whose land they have hunted during the winter.

The sport has thrived in recent years. The season, which begins on the second Saturday in February and can run until early June, comprised 199 meetings at 113 courses during 1990. The courses, spread throughout the country, range from such as Larkhill and Tweseldown, which race regularly, to about 50 courses which have just one meeting.

There is a strong connection between point-to-pointing and hunting. To qualify to run in point-to-points, horses must be granted a certificate which proves them to have been 'properly and fairly hunted'. The certificates must then be registered with Weatherbys so that the Jockey Club, which oversees point-to-point racing, is aware of those horses which are qualified.

That description is something of a grey area, and is decided between the Master of the Hunt in question and the owners of the horse. There is no stipulation as to the number of times a horse must have hunted before it can be qualified, largely because the geographical conditions can vary greatly from area to area. Some hunts, for example, which operate in suburban parts, cannot hunt frequently because of the restrictions of road traffic. More rural hunts will be able to turn out with greater freedom.

Many horses spend their lives in point-to-point races, but there is a route through to hunter chases. They are run on racecourses under Jockey Club rules which apply to every other area of racing. The hunter's certificate applies to both point-to-points and hunter chases, but to race in hunter chases owners must be registered, as must colours and so on. Such regulations do not apply to point-to-pointing. Riders must also be licensed under Jockey Club rules.

The Jockey Club's rules on ownership do not apply in point-to-points. For example, partnerships do not have to be registered, although the partners have to be associated with a hunt.

Although the majority of point-to-point owners are hunting orientated, or farmers, there is a growing number of people who are not directly concerned with hunting becoming involved. However, those owners must still be a member of a hunt, even if they themselves do not ride the horse. For someone without the land to keep the horse himself, the usual route is to put the horse in a livery yard, which is, basically, somewhere to board it.

Some sections of the sport are reluctant to recognise, officially, that livery yard proprietors are, in many cases, acting as trainers of point-to-pointers, because it contravenes the spirit of what is considered an amateur sport. However, the fact is that some livery yards are training establishments, although on a much reduced scale compared to mainstream racing.

Fees, as with training stables, will vary considerably, rising to around £120 in the leading livery yards. Given that hunting begins several months before the season starts – to get the horses qualified – and that horses have a month after the end of the season to wind down before being turned out to grass, a point-to-pointer will be in livery for about eight months of the year.

Total prize-money per race is usually a maximum of £175, although some categories of event may go up to £250. That, remember, is total prize-money, the winner's share being only a proportion of that figure. Point-to-point prize-money has been boosted by sponsorship (notably from Land Rover, RMC and *The Times*) in which a series of qualifying races culminate in

Point-to-point racing

a hunter chase final on a racecourse proper.

Although the costs of keeping a point-to-pointer will be lower than for a racehorse in training, the prospects of making it pay are similar – extremely slim.

Making entries for point-to-points requires a certain amount of forward planning. Point-to-point entries close a week before the meeting, so it is important that the hunter's certificate has been lodged in good time for qualification. Expect to pay about £8 per entry, which should then be sent to the entry secretary for each meeting.

Point-to-pointers are mostly former racehorses or young horses being brought along gradually. Buying a potential point-to-pointer requires no less care than the purchase of any other horse. More, perhaps, because it is being used for a specific purpose. The demands of point-to-pointing require a chasing type: strength, soundness and stamina are the necessary qualities. A whippet-like former Flat racer is an unlikely candidate.

A horse's attitude is also important. It may often be ridden by an inexperienced pilot, perhaps even a member of the family, so avoid those which jump badly and which take a strong hold. Race-riding is dangerous enough without sitting on a time-bomb. Steady, experienced chasers can be a safer bet as schoolmasters, although for the 1991 season, horses which have won a steeple-chase, except an amateur riders' race, worth more than £7,500 in the previous three seasons are ineligible for point-to-points and hunter chases. The rule was introduced to prevent high-class chasers joining the point-to-point ranks and picking off prizes at will.

The hunting fraternity is, however, quite capable of producing its own top-class performers. The Dikler, the winner of the 1973 Cheltenham Gold Cup, progressed through point-to-points, as did Grittar, the 1982 Grand National winner. The 1989–90 National Hunt season proved to be a bonanza for point-to-point old boys. Norton's Coin, the Cheltenham Gold Cup winner, and Mr Frisk, successful in the Grand National, had both raced in point-to-points in previous years.

Horses can be sold with a hunter's certificate good for one season only. New qualifications must be obtained for each

131

succeeding season.

There is a qualification to ride in point-to-points, but it has nothing to do with ability. A rider must have a Riders' Qualification Certificate, which, going back to the hunting link, must be issued by the Hunt Secretary, rather than the Master. All the certificate does is establish the rider's link with the Hunt. The Jockey Club advises secretaries to exercise caution in giving out licences, but there is no rule governing fitness to ride.

Point-to-point racing is embraced by its devotees as a good afternoon out. Admission is usually by car, regardless of the number of passengers, rather than by person. Facilities are more spartan than on racecourses, but there is usually some cover, and liquid refreshment of all varieties, to be had. Fixtures are advertised in *The Sporting Life*, although several national newspapers now carry a list, with directions, on race-days.

The novice should choose a day when the weather smiles. Shivering through a wet afternoon and then having to call upon the services of a tractor to pull your car out of a quagmire will kill the interest of all but the most hardened enthusiast.

Useful addresses

The Jockey Club
42 Portman Square
London W1H 0EN

Federation of Bloodstock
Agents (GB) Ltd
The Old Brewery
Hampton Street
Tetbury
Gloucestershire
GL8 8PG

Jockeys' Association
1 Bridge Street
Newbury
Berkshire RG14 5BL

National Trainers' Federation
42 Portman Square
London W1H 0AP

Racecourse Association
Winkfield Road
Ascot
Berkshire
SL5 7HX

Racehorse Owners' Association
42 Portman Square
London W1H 9FF

Thoroughbred Breeders'
Association
Stanstead House
The Avenue
Newmarket
Suffolk
CB8 9AA

Weatherbys
Sanders Road
Wellingborough
Northants
NN8 4BX

Pratt & Co
11 Boltro Road
Haywards Heath
Sussex RH16 1BP

Summary of registration charges 1990
(exclusive of VAT)

	£
Of an owner	29.00
Colours	15.00
Of a name	
Under two-year-olds	16.50
Two- and three-years-old	33.00
Four-years-old and upwards	27.50
Change of name	140.00
Reservation of name	16.50
Of training agreement	4.50
Of authority to act	19.50
Of a club	75.00
Of a company	275.00
Of a partnership	16.50
Of a partnership name	55.00
Of a lease	16.50

THE
BRILLIANTLY SUCCESSFUL

FULL CIRCLE

MANAGED BY COLIN TINKLER
THE LEADERS IN GROUP OWNERSHIP